LONDON OVERLOOKED

ALSO BY GEOFFREY FLETCHER

Town's Eye View

The London Nobody Knows

City Sights

Frontispiece : The Old Bedford, 1964

LONDON
OVERLOOKED

*

WRITTEN AND ILLUSTRATED BY

Geoffrey S. Fletcher

HUTCHINSON OF LONDON

HUTCHINSON & CO (*Publishers*) LTD

178–202 Great Portland Street, London, W.1

London Melbourne Sydney
Auckland Bombay Toronto
Johannesburg New York

★

First published 1964

© Geoffrey S. Fletcher 1964

This book has been set in Monophoto Ehrhardt. It has been printed in Great Britain by William Clowes and Sons, Ltd.,
London and Beccles

To
Jean and Rags

———— ✳ ————

Contents

ONE

The Magic of the Halls [1]

————————— * —————————

OF ALL the rich and picturesque institutions connected with Metropolitan life,
there are few more appealing than the London Music Hall. Up to a comparatively
recent period, these entertainments were as natural a part of the working Londoner's leisure hours as Epsom on Derby Day, Hampstead on August Bank
Holiday or the Welsh Harp on a summer Sunday morning. At such places as the
Middlesex in Drury Lane, on the site now occupied by the Winter Garden
theatre, itself soon to disappear, the sumptuous Canterbury or the rougher, less
lavish establishments like the Foresters, London working men and women could
momentarily escape from the drabness of crowded rooms in mean streets, hear
and join in their favourite songs during a long, cheap evening in a glowing gold,
plushy interior as unlike their normal surroundings as could be imagined: gaslight and gaiety effectively combined. The artistes, most of whom had originated
from the same background, knew precisely what was required of them. All these
elements – architectural and human, musical and pictorial – fused to make the
most extraordinary form of art created by London.

But those pale-faced Londoners, illuminated by the footlights under chin,
nose and eye-sockets, sporting Cokes and Derbys, accompanied by their Donahs,
who peer through gallery railings in Sickert's paintings were unconscious of the
music hall's being a form of art. If any intellectual had assured them that it was
so, they would have been scornful and incredulous: to them the halls offered a
relief to lives even more humdrum than ours of the present day; the pub con-
stituted a similar aid. Pubs were among the mixed ancestry of the music hall, an
association often preserved by an architectural relationship, as at Collins's, the
Washington and many others. Pub and music hall were both illusions, of course,
but no more than the ideas of progress fostered by the politicians or the vision by
the churchmen of the good time coming. The human comedy itself, the basic
material used by the music hall, is only a make-believe, badly acted by stale
comics shouting at the tops of their voices to distract themselves from the darkness outside.

The great historical period of the music hall was from 1850 to 1900. That half-century saw it emerging from the entertainments of the bar, the song and supper rooms such as Evans's (in the eighteenth-century mansion still in existence as a fruiterer's warehouse on the north side of Covent Garden) and the miscellaneous concert rooms where turns were added as an extra inducement to the serious business of consuming food and drink. The Dr. Johnson Tavern in Bolt Court, Fleet Street, long since extinct, was typical of the genre. The tavern was famous for its brown beer, kidneys and chops and oysters: no charge was made for admission to the concert room. Rustic and bucolic songs were the entertainments mainly offered: it was in the song saloons, before the music hall had established itself in its own right, that the earliest artistes made their début – Jenny Hill, the Vital Spark, for instance, first appeared at this tavern.

Tavern saloons of this kind, contained either within the building or in the gardens at the rear (the Apollo Saloon behind the Yorkshire Stingo in Marylebone was an example of the latter), began to appear in great numbers all over London about the time of Victoria's accession. The Rose of Normandy, rebuilt later in the century, still exists in Marylebone High Street, and is now used by the B.B.C. Others include the Eagle (also known as the Grecian) in the City Road, the King and Queen near Paddington Green, the Lansdowne Arms, Islington, later to grow into the famous Collins's Music Hall, and the Mogul or 'Old Mo' which became the Middlesex.

Charles Morton has been considered the father of the London music hall, though he largely carried out ideas already in the air. He determined to introduce the type of entertainments in demand at Evans's to his own pub, the Canterbury Arms, in what is now the Westminster Bridge Road. This was in the late 1840's; the idea was successful and led immediately to the building of a separate hall. The music of Offenbach was first popularized here. Other attractions included the singer Sam Cowell, and E. W. Mackney, an early 'coon' type vocalist. As might be expected, the variety and singing turns were the most appreciated; the operatic items were gradually eliminated, and another, more lavish Canterbury was built, with a horse-shoe auditorium and a balcony.

Of this first phase of the music hall, only two examples survive in London in a complete state, as far as I am aware – Macdonald's in Hoxton and Wilton's in Wellclose Square. It is difficult to decide which kind to admire more – the simplicity of the early period, of which the slender cast iron columns and delicate balcony of Macdonald's, illustrated opposite, serves as a central type, or the richness associated with the later phase of rebuilding in halls of increased size of the 1890's. But the later halls had lost one feature essential, in my opinion, to the true character of the halls – the marble-topped tables had disappeared to make way for extra seats in pit and stalls, the booze was relegated to bars and a subtle change of emphasis in the halls of the 'nineties gave more scope to variety acts,

Early music Hall instrumental

Hoxton

whereas the bills of the 'sixties, 'seventies and 'eighties were more vocal and comic: beer and songs go as naturally together as Cain and Abel, cheese and onions.

From the stage of the Canterbury, George Leybourne, the first 'Lion Comique', drove the music hall population of London crazy with his

> Champagne Charlie is my name,
> Yes, Champagne Charlie is my name.
> Good for any game at night, boys,
> Champagne Charlie is my name.

On this song and others of a similar kind, Leybourne rapidly rose to the top of the 'profession', like one of his own champagne corks. He used to drive to the Canterbury in a brougham drawn by four white horses – an excellent advertisement, like the drinking songs themselves. Off stage, Leybourne lived a life little different in character from his own Champagne Charlie, with whom he became identified: the masher or heavy swell – the mid-Victorian equivalent, almost, of the Regency buck and ancestor, nearly, of the Piccadilly Johnnie. Concanen's song cover of Leybourne tapping a champagne bottle with his cane, like many other song covers of this period, realizes the 'swell' completely – both on and off stage. Concanen is too interesting to pass over quickly, and I shall return to him later.

The final and most sumptuous Canterbury was opened in 1876. Besides a picture gallery, fernery and promenade, the Canterbury, like the Bedford, had a sliding roof for pleasant ventilation on summer nights. An open cindered space marks the site of the Canterbury today, a parking area for the transport of St. Thomas's Hospital between the flats and the railway arches. The fragments which remain, illustrated on page 31, are worth the pilgrimage, by the side of the arches down Carlisle Lane. The entrance to the Canterbury ran under the railway arches, a long tunnel lined with mosaics that connected the entrance in Westminster Bridge Road with the auditorium. Some of these mosaics in duck egg blue and gold still remain, though rapidly crumbling from the damp tunnel walls. How it was the rumble of the railway never interfered with Canterbury entertainments I am unable to guess. At the end of the tunnel the outline of stone steps can be seen yet and part of the walls lettered with the words 'To Circle and Gallery' with a hand now pointing only to the sky. Behind the transport drivers' hut is a portion of the panelled walls of one side of the music hall. Soon even these melancholy fragments will be gone.

From the Canterbury, Morton moved on to build the Oxford on a site now occupied by Lyons' Oxford Street Corner House. The first Oxford (the hall was rebuilt on more than one occasion) opened in 1861 and contained a supper room and promenade bars. By this time, the early 'sixties, music halls were appearing all over London: the Alhambra in Leicester Square, where Leotard (the original of Leybourne's 'Daring Young Man on the Flying Trapeze') appeared, careering above the audience without the moral support of a safety net; the Metropolitan, the Bedford and many others, nearly all in working-class districts.

Strong nerves and determination are necessary for the solitary exploration of the derelict London halls. Apart from the risk of falling masonry or the breaking of one's neck on ruined staircases, there are other discomforts incidental to such explorations in the shape of tramps, dead or alive or with one foot in the grave, and rats. Moreover, left alone in these places where the plaster masks smile down on scenes of absolute decay, one has a disagreeable knack of recalling various stories of odd happenings in London theatres – the ghostly hands at the St. James's or the noises and sinister opening doors Lew Lake used to talk about at Collins's. I recently revisited the derelict Bedford after the lapse of several years on a day matched to the purpose, one of lowering dark clouds and heavy rain. The sudden view of the ruined auditorium from back stage was infinitely melancholy and depressing. I picked my way gingerly across the stage where great gaps in the slippery boards disclosed a depth of several feet of filthy water in the mezzanine below the joists. The safety curtain hung in shreds, flapping eerily, like the banner of some hopeless cause, in the wind that moaned through that deserted place. Rain poured steadily through a hole in what was once a charming coved ceiling – I think the Bedford was the prettiest hall in London – not an elaborate ceiling like the Metropolitan's, but a simple, elegant arrangement of mouldings and plain surfaces. The first Bedford (the one with the sliding roof) opened in September 1861; the present Bedford dates from the 'nineties. Sickert painted both. The seats had long disappeared, so had the charming *art nouveau* caryatids, all but the top half of one which still supported the plaster draperies of the adjoining box (illustrated on page 15). Those solid-looking nymphs, columns and archivolts were nothing but plaster and jute: time had dealt severely with their pretensions and shown them to be an elegant sham.

On the floor, among the crumbling plaster ornaments, lay a long dead Christmas tree. Tramps had taken nightly shelter in the music hall, leaving their stinking rags on the floor, along with their shit. Down-and-outs had evidently occupied the boxes, possibly the only time they had ever indulged in the luxury, and flies, surely the least fastidious of the creatures of God (less than men and women even), crawled over the excreta. The plaster was almost gone from the fronts of gallery and circle, showing the fireproof construction underneath, but the two supporting figures on top of the proscenium arch, one each side of the coat-of-arms, were intact, as were the four cupids, two on each side above the boxes.

I explored the dark staircases and passages by the light of a small torch; from the gods the derelict interior appeared even more melancholy than from below. Suddenly, turning round in the dark, I saw the outline of a figure moving about behind a door in the gallery and felt my pulse missing a beat, several beats. Fortunately it was my own figure, reflected in the glass of a door in the gloom, but it was an undesirable sensation while it lasted. Empty theatres are always full of strange sounds – muffled footfalls, whisperings – and to listen to the moaning of the wind, the beating of the rain and of one's own heart in the darkened gallery of an abandoned music hall where doors mysteriously open and shut is not pleasant. I wondered if, after all, I was not alone, if I had company besides the ginger cat I saw stalking across the stage – visitors who ought to be resting. And I thought of Belle Elmore. The murder of Belle Elmore was a crime with a complete music hall background. She appeared at the Bedford, on this same stage, quite often – a throw-away turn. She was a Jewess, fond of jewelry, and Crippen (that wonderfully sinister Crippen with the heavy moustache) gave her plenty. Marie Lloyd's sharp eyes recognized some of the pieces being worn at a Variety ball, and reported her suspicions to Scotland Yard. . . . Altogether I was glad when my work was done, and I was able to return to Camden High Street, where the air is delicately perfumed with petrol and beefburgers, where every night is a frying night and negroes shore up the fronts of the shops selling swish clothes.

I had a similar experience at the Star, Bermondsey, one of the most famous, as well as among the toughest, of those 'on the Surrey side'. Here Bessie Bellwood, whose life away from the footlights was notably daredevil and Bohemian, made her first appearance. Marie Lloyd appeared here in her early days and Tom "Percy from Pimlico" Leamore, but the Star is chiefly associated with Leo Dryden and his songs of Empire – eminently 'The Miner's Dream of Home'. Dryden died in obscurity, with little to his name, as did so many of the stars who had either spent all they got or were overtaken by changing tastes, left high and dry when the music hall had entered into its decline. An L.C.C. official opened up the Star for me, by appointment, locking me in while he went off on another assignment, for, as he said, 'You might have tramps getting in. In fact, you may find a dead one here already.' Hobos were missing on that day, but as I made my drawing, I heard the rustling and squeaking of the rats, the only remaining audience in the gloom below, among the rags left by the last occupiers.

The Star has now been demolished, along with the contemporary pub adjoining, the Star and Garter. I have recorded the exterior in the drawing on page 17. The façade was cut brick and carefully built; white brick was used as a contrast. The columns at the entrance had Byzantine-type basket capitals. This Eastern touch often occurred in music hall architecture: the Alhambra was the most remarkable example, and the foyer of the Metropolitan was 'Moorish', the rest of the interior being Baroque. As the nineteenth century progressed, music

The ruins of
the prompt side box of the Bedford.
G S Dalrhope May 1962.

hall architecture became a job for specialists, such as Albert Bridgeman and Frank Matcham. London theatre architects supplied many of the plans for the provincial halls.

The interior of the Star was very simply arranged. It was small in scale, with an upper and a lower balcony and arcaded walls. The balcony fronts – this is characteristic of much early work – were of delicate cast iron, each forming a continuous horseshoe band, supported on thin iron columns. The proscenium arch, unusually high for its width, was ornamented with a diaper pattern. The Star became a cinema for years, though it still staged its annual pantomime until the war, when the place closed down completely.

One of the most delightful of the earlier halls, Wilton's, illustrated on page 25, remains in Grace's Alley, Wellclose Square, Stepney, in remarkably good preservation. At the moment, the place is used by Coppermills, rag dealers (music halls seem to have a fatal attraction for rags), but I should like to see the place restored again and used, with some of the many rooms displaying music halls relics – playbills, photographs and whatnot. Few passing the pretty entrance, carved with fruits and flowers on each side of the jambs, could guess the extent of the interior arrangements. The auditorium is rectangular; the single balcony, supported by barley sugar columns, is rounded at the corners farthest from the stage, forming a 'U' shape on plan. A continuous band of plaster having an 'S' section forms the balcony front, decorated with swags and acanthus foliage in moderately low relief. Along the walls are pilasters from which spring arches – two to a bay meeting on a console, or bracket, midway between the pilasters. The ceiling is a shallow barrel vault, having a depressed curve; richly ornamented ribs, still largely in good condition, run down on to the pilasters. At the opposite end to the stage is an apsidal shallow bay, and below this is (or was, since the bales of waste rags make proper examination a matter of difficulty) the famous Mahogany Bar. The number of subsidiary rooms is a curiosity of Wilton's; quite possibly the owner lived on the premises. One room – that to the right of the entrance on the ground floor, adjoining the staircase (this, by the way, has cast iron newel posts and a mahogany handrail) possesses an elaborate plaster lintel, a Rococo panel on a wall and a carved cornice above the door with a Lear-like head in the centre. There are traces of the original wall paper, lithographed in two or three shades of brown and buff, below the later wooden dados. Near the stairs is the foundation stone 'laid by Ellen wife of John Wilton on Thursday the 9th day of December 1858'; the theatre was opened, I believe, in the following year.

The speed at which many of the halls were built and equipped is very remarkable in view of the craftsmanship put into them. Wilton's closed in 1879, at a time when the finest period of the halls was commencing. A visit to Wilton's ought to wind up by threading a way through greasy, dimly lit streets (a man was

the Star Music Hall
Abbey St. Bermondsey.

found murdered in the basement of a café a stone's throw from Wilton's after my last visit, though the two were unconnected), past working men's lodgings and the great, grim C.W.S. offices to Aldgate to indulge in winkles – champagne, too, if you are properly equipped – and whelks at one of the stalls by Petticoat Lane. Many of the older halls had stages of remarkably little depth – Wilton's and Macdonald's, Hoxton, being two halls where this can still be seen. The scenery was nominal, relying mainly on the painted backdrop of rural subjects or those empty town streets where it always seemed Sunday afternoon. Oil and gas lamps were, of course, the illuminants at this period: one of the best shots in Tommy Trinder's film *Champagne Charlie* – in which he played the part of George Leybourne singing round the town against his rival, the Great Vance – was of the naked gas flares, protected only by wire netting, in the wings.

Mention of Tommy Trinder brings me to the Metropolitan and that memorable last night there with Ida Barr, Dorothy Ward, Shaun Glenville, Wee Georgie Wood – and Ada Reeve, whose memories of the music hall are long and enlightening. (She first appeared at Gattis-under-the-arches, now the Players, in 1888.) One of them is too rich to omit and concerns the washing facilities at the Marylebone, which, as she has told me, consisted mainly of a bucket of water. This bucket was passed under the curtain which served to divide the men's from the women's quarters; only, in Ada Reeve's words, 'we girls had sometimes used it for other purposes. . . .' Without doubt, the Metropolitan was the richest example of the late Victorian music hall in London, and its disappearance in favour of one of the endless road schemes now eating away London is a matter of infinite regret. The theatre had been kept going as a music hall somehow or other, with the addition of wrestling and bingo sessions; but for the road scheme, the theatre might have survived long enough to become a protected building. It is one of the follies of contemporary London that no such attempt has yet been made.

An ancient hostelry dating from 1525, the White Lion in Edgware Road, occupied the site of the Metropolitan; its concert room was improved in 1862 into a music hall, known as Turnham's Grand Concert Rooms, which became the Metropolitan Music Hall in 1864, with a final rebuilding in 1897, to the designs of Frank Matcham. Every square foot of the Metropolitan was the purest music hall Baroque, from the brilliantly tiled pit bar to the ceiling decorations stained by time and smoke to the colour of an old violin. Caryatid figures, male and female, supported the boxes on either side of the stage, incidentally forming stock subjects for comedian's patter. The illustration opposite of one of those heads and the surrounding plaster decorations conveys a little of the rich effect. Also from the Metropolitan is the drawing on page 35 of one of the two gigantic winged females of the gods, who smilingly, and without apparent effort, carried their

INTERVAL

The Metropolitan

share of the ceiling on dusty shoulders through long years, receiving gleams of gold from the footlights on their tarnished wings. And then, those denizens of the gods themselves – peering at odd angles through the brass rails, pink blobs for faces against a brown and tobacco smoke background.

> The boy I love sits up in the gallery,
> The boy I love is looking down at me,
> Can't you see, there he is, a-waving of his handkerchief
> As merry as a robin that sings on a tree

sung by Nellie Power, Little Dot Hetherington and your own, your very own, Miss Marie Lloyd.

As a living music hall is an amalgam of music and light, people and florid decoration, enveloped in a lively atmosphere that can be sensed even after the audience has gone, it is no wonder that other entertainments – plays, films or what-you-will – fit but uneasily in a 'hall'. Nights of bingo and wrestling were, of course, wildly out of character, but there was at least one period touch during a wrestling match at the Met. when, from his seat in the front row of the stalls, an angry old man (angry old men being infinitely preferable to angry new ones as a source of entertainment) belaboured a wrestler soundly on the back with an umbrella. Moreover, during the weeks when I was recording the building inside and out, I used to amuse myself by studying the doodlings of the bingo patrons – women mostly – on the smooth side of the hardboard pads lent to them as a support. Lack of training in psychology prevented my interpreting the numerous scribbles of breasts, cubes and rhomboids; still, one message was a cry from the heart, 'Oh, God, help me to win'.

I mentioned Collins's very briefly in *The London Nobody Knows*. A little more can, I think, be added here as a sort of valedictory footnote, if only because the 'Chapel on the Green' has disappeared, all but the façade, since the publication of my previous book. Sam Collins, 'the inimitable Irish vocalist', died in 1865 aged thirty-nine. Early death was a professional hazard on the variety stage of the Victorian era. Collins, who had been in management before, took over the Lansdowne Music Hall in 1862, rebuilding it as Collins's during 1863, with an adjoining pub still known as the Lansdowne. Collins's followed the general pattern with a rebuilding in the late 'nineties. The Lansdowne continued to function as a pub after the fire which put an end to the effort to keep Collins's open. In the end the whole site was required for other purposes and the Lansdowne had to go. Those last few evenings before New Year's Eve 1962 were tinged with depression: dissolution was round the corner and the very paper chains left over from Christmas sagged dejectedly. In June 1963 I was there to record the demolition of both pub and music hall (illustrated on page 33). Dirt and dust lay thick in the arched, lincrusta papered passage that led to the pay box – an entrance once, as I remembered, crowded with galleryites on a Saturday night, the more wealthy having paid for the privilege of 'early doors', which, being interpreted, meant a head start in the scramble for those Olympian benches where the fish-tail gas jets flickered in their cages of wire. The Edwardian wall-paper was peeling off in the passage, disclosing a stencilled pattern underneath – evidently that applied when Collins's was rebuilt in the 'nineties. A notice dug up from the past announced that 'owing to present conditions, children's prams and babies in arms could no longer be admitted free of charge'. What conditions were those that could bring on such a massacre of the innocents? The auditorium was desolate. Only the proscenium arch remained, its cupids looking down on tons of brickwork and cement rubble where the stalls had been. (The death of a theatre is a fearful sight: I felt as depressed as I had been when watching the demolition of St. James's, with a great fire reflecting on that golden arch under which Oscar Wilde and Rachel had stood.) Men with oxyacetylene burners were cutting up the exposed girders, once part of the circle – the gods having completely disappeared. Collins's was open to the sky. The bar was a mass of woodwork, piled on the floor, a confused jumble of carved capitals, metal and brick. The Lansdowne was turned into a temporary office for the contractors' men, but bits of the Christmas paper chains still clung to the ceiling. Clean patches on the walls of the bar showed where the playbills, sold by auction, had hung. An old photograph of Lew Lake lay in the dust trampled underfoot; someone had added a pencilled moustache. Before leaving, I had a last look. I stood on the piles of debris, watching the bricks fall in clouds of choking mortar dust. As I watched, there was a crack of thunder fit to rouse the dead who lie in the old, forgotten graveyard below the music hall, and torrential rain swept over the rubble. Suddenly, as if aware of their cue, the plaster cupids heeled over, disintegrating as they fell, and became part of the shapeless mass below.

The immense popularity of the halls led to the introduction of music hall items in the legitimate theatre. Sadler's Wells, the Standard at Shoreditch, the Surrey and the Old Vic were a few of the 'regular' playhouses where variety acts were included in Shakespearian productions, slipped in between melodramas and farces. The Britannia at Hoxton, today an empty space in the High Street, with a little stonework surviving on each side, indulged in this for many years under the direction of its famous actress-manageress, Mrs. Sara Lane. The staple diet at the Britannia was barnstorming melodrama of Sweeney Todd flavour. At Christmas came the famous pantomimes still lovingly remembered by old Londoners. After my drawing of Macdonald's Music Hall appeared in the *Daily Telegraph* in 1963, I had a letter from an old lady which gave so graphic an account of that old life of London – Hoxton was suburban then – that I cannot deny myself the pleasure of transcribing it: '. . . the famous Britannia Theatre with the largest stage in London and once owned by the well-loved Sara Lane. I remember being taken seventy years ago to see the Pantomimes there, with their Harlequinade and wonderful transformation scenes. One year a monstrous garden on the stage reaching high up towards the roof, and as the lights changed, the flowers moved forward and opened to reveal many lovely girls, some of whom seemed to fly out over the Orchestra Pit. Another year the scene appeared to be a gigantic fire-work display, which was really dozens of fountains with coloured changing lights being played on them. The programme assured us that the water was used over and again, and none was wasted. Theatres today show us nothing to equal these displays. Later I remember seeing the Melville Brothers (or was it The Walter Melville) Dramas – *Ten Days' Leave*, *East Lynne*, *The Crimes of Paris*. This play had a working lift on the stage in one act. There were many others, the names I can't remember now. But I do remember their regular company, Roy Redgrave (The Hero), Beatrice Toye with her deep voice (The Heroine), Algernon Sims (The Villain whom we hissed lustily whenever he appeared on the stage) . . . all for fourpence in the gallery and a shilling in the pit.'

A Crummles-type theatre which turned to music hall items was the Royal West London, the portico of which, now a parking place for flyposters, still remains in Church Street, Edgware Road. A drawing of this portico is reproduced opposite; the rest of the theatre was destroyed by fire. When the street market is in session, piles of vegetables, old furniture and household requisites almost reach the lintel, for this is no majestic portico of Attic grandeur, it is only the lowly, home-made Doric of the shabby little London streets. This portico dates from about 1837. The theatre underwent many changes of management and ownership with as many fluctuations of fortune and changes of name, 'The Royal Marylebone Theatre' and 'Theatre Royal Marylebone' among them. Farces, patriotic pieces, improvised adaptations from popular novelists appeared to-gether with the musical items and dog-dramas – sagacious dogs performed feats of devotion in these canine pieces, the hapless human actors being, of course, mere stooges whose presence was tolerated merely on account of the plot. The playhouse was gutted during the last war. Its entrance has survived simply, I suppose, because no one has bothered to knock it down, but it will disappear eventually. Meanwhile the local dogs, mindful perhaps of their ancestors' great times, continue to go there, for reasons entirely private.

Macdonald's Music Hall in Hoxton is fortunately one of the few survivors not threatened with demolition. This part of Shoreditch is full of character and interest for the London perambulator and will be described in a later chapter. Macdonald's owes its continued existence to the fact that it became a mission hall. It remains so to this day as a centre for Quaker social service. Macdonald's is

The Royal West London

a short distance from the site of the Britannia and opposite the Bacchus (what better name for a pub?). Behind a nondescript entrance is probably the finest surviving hall (apart from Wilton's) of the early Vance-Leybourne period. It has all the qualities of the emerging music hall – small, intimate, with an almost classic simplicity. Plain walls are a feature of the early halls, a simplicity of treatment that allowed the delicate ironwork of balconies and supporting columns to be seen to advantage.

The old entrance front, no longer used, is in Wilk's Place, the date 1863 being carved on the keystone. The original doors remain; one leads to the cellars beneath the hall. A century ago, Macdonald's was surrounded by small shops, with a cowshed and dairy immediately adjoining. (Genuine dairies, by the way, with cows kept on the premises, lingered on until a late period in London. There was one in Chelsea up to 1914 and one in Islington until the 1920's.) Slender iron columns topped with acanthus capitals support the first gallery. Those of the upper gallery are simpler. The walls of the auditorium are panelled with blank arcades which run down on to fluted pilasters. Two panels, edged like a Victorian valentine, form the only decorative feature; these once held mirrors. Below the panels were the couple of cast iron stoves that served to heat the hall – the rest of the warmth, presumably, being supplied by the audience themselves. The original colour scheme can only be guessed at, for underneath the present white are brown and green layers and gold underneath that. White or cream and gold, the colour scheme of Wilton's, seems a reasonable supposition.

The stage appears to have its original steps on each side; certainly the door midway in the wall back stage remains intact. What has gone is the plaster ceiling which, destroyed during the last war, was replaced by a plaster board affair. Something of the old music hall entertainments is kept going at Macdonald's, where the ladies of Hoxton gather for sing-songs. Many of these songs are survivals from an early date, having remained intact in what students of social history term 'the folk memory'. By a process similar to that which mysteriously hands down the games of school children, the people of Hoxton have preserved a few of the genuine street ballads of London. One deals with the gates of London, ending up at Newgate, a name that vanished from the consciousness of most Londoners when Newgate Prison was demolished early in the present century to make way for the Central Criminal Court. During my last visit, however, these excellent dames were more up to date with a barndance and 'Maybe it's because I'm a Londoner'. Then there was 'The Lily of Laguna' and Harry Champion's 'Any Old Iron': letting down their grey hair, so to speak, the old girls of Hoxton – thin or fat, rheumaticky or otherwise – pounded the floor, weaving in and out of the cast iron columns (those same columns that had once heard Victor Liston and Fred Albert), cheered on by the ladies who were sitting round the hall.

Wilton's
Music Hall
Wellclose Square

In this incomplete review of the London halls, I have omitted to mention those that came later in the suburbs, such as the Golders Green Hippodrome, the Hackney Empire and the Wood Green Empire. Although I hope as many as possible will escape demolition, I have never been able to consider them in the same light as those older halls of central London and the East End. Plush and gold they may have, but not the long tradition of public house entertainment and concert room behind them. Moreover, when the later halls appeared in what were then raw suburban areas, the music hall tradition was changing into variety – a much more miscellaneous entertainment, largely purged of the earthiness and bucolic crudity of the earlier time, the period vividly recorded in the countless drawings and many paintings of Sickert.

Most of the present-day attempts to revive the music hall, even in those nearest in character – I mean the entertainments of the so-called music hall pubs, overlook the fact that the music hall was primarily an affair of the London working class, of which only a few representatives remain, largely in the East End. That old type of Londoner – industrious, not given to complaining over much, with his own traditional enjoyments, living all his life in one small section of a great city, aware of the folly of expecting too much from life, possessing a humour tinged with melancholy – disappeared during the Great War or shortly after, having seen more than was good for him. His disappearance coincided with the growth of the cinema, the increasing importation of American ideas and many other factors affecting the London halls. Fortunately the music hall itself had taken his portrait in a number of incomparable songs – the Cockney and his Donah, born not exactly within the sound of Bow Bells but representing the absolute spirit of yesterday's London nonetheless. Pre-eminently, I think, comes Albert Chevalier's 'The Future Mrs. 'Awkins', a masterpiece of rough but tender sentiment with an underlying note of pathos or yearning. Liza – the Mrs. 'Awkins that was to be – was drawn on many occasions by Phil May, the counterpart, in pictorial art, of Chevalier; Nicholson drew her portrait exactly in his colour woodcut called 'Hammersmith'. Gus Elen with his postmen and dustmen preserved the more lugubrious aspect of Cockneydom, types long since vanished but known to Dickens and Cruikshank. Marie Lloyd with her 'Coster Girl in Paris' did the same: Kate Carney's song 'Three Pots a Shilling' comes to mind and many more – a continuing tradition from 'Sally in our Alley', 'The Ratcatcher's Daughter' and 'Polly Perkins' up to the Great War, when, as I have suggested, the Cockney was absorbed in the anonymous mass which, hedged in with disciplinary laws and almost entirely characterless, we now call Londoners.

Probably at the time (the late 1890's), the substitution of the beer-swigging, cigar-smoking chairman was held to be an improvement: it was in fact a part of a slow decline, for the disappearance of that functionary was accompanied by other signs of modernization – the acceptance of the two houses a night system and the moving pictures tacked on at the end of the programme. Wonderful pictorial pleasures were part of the charm of the older halls of London: the striking reflections in mirrors, foregrounds of billycock hats, hands appearing out of the orchestra pit, fingering 'cellos or playing the soulful flageolet, a few women's bonnets (men were in a majority), pipes and glasses, curving balconies, light on gilded cornices: and that chairman himself, not in the vaguely Regency outfit inaccurately favoured by the chairmen of present-day revivals, but in ordinary evening dress, displaying a broad shirt front and flashy pin, watch-chain over waistcoat, buttonhole and a large ring and cigar. Around him, seated at marble tables were the audience, enjoying their porter or half and half, smoking clay pipes and joining in the choruses. To sit at the table occupied by the chairman was considered choice and enabled you to buy that great official a drink. Hopeful waiters hovered round the tables ready to oblige, shouting above the smoke, gaslight and din, the encouraging words, 'Hany horders? Give your horders, gents, please!'

TWO

The Magic of the Halls [2]

———— ✳ ————

ONE OF the handicaps to writing on London is the speed at which demolitions take place, so that a book may well be dated before publication. This applies especially to the music halls, or anything else in the way of progress towards the uniform, highly industrialized, processed society being imposed on us. However, no doubt a few music halls will remain in London, turned over to other uses – memorials, along with the churches, of a vanished civilization as mysterious and incomprehensible in the coming time as Stonehenge. That music halls represented a rich phase of London life is without doubt and it is equally true that the music hall was a purely London innovation, however quickly and successfully extended to the provinces. It was one of the few authentic forms of popular art to spring from the working class and one that contained many poetic qualities, albeit intermingled with meaner elements. Such music halls as may survive are worth regular study on the part of all who care for the old London. Buildings of this kind will most assuredly never appear again. It is unfortunate that most of the skill of their architects was employed on creating enchanting interiors; the street elevations were of less account. Two or three more halls remain to be mentioned out of the great number that once existed in London.

Shoreditch, including its parish of Hoxton, was unusually strong in minor theatres, music halls and singsongs. It was, of course, just outside the reach of City magistrates. Two of the most famous halls have now gone, but their sites can be visited in a tour that can take in those still in existence. One was the Olympia in Bishopsgate, facing the goods yard. Its site can be determined precisely for the Olympia stood exactly opposite a candelabra-like gas lamp on a tall stone pillar, which, by some oversight, has been allowed to remain though denuded of its lamps. The Olympia had a recessed upper storey, topped by a heavy Classical cornice, with an arcaded portico below. It resembled, in fact, the more expensive Wesleyan churches of the mid-nineteenth century. A splendid iron and glass porch or covered way ran from portico to kerb, almost identical to the one still remaining outside the Palace, Cambridge Circus.

Still more famous and often visited by Sickert was the London, Shoreditch, opened in 1892. Only a brick wall now remains, adjoining St. Leonard's Church; there is a car park in the foreground, with the wall in the distance, by the side of the premises of Jeremiah Rotherham & Company. Two others in the neighbourhood were the St. Leonard's Hall, almost opposite the church, and the Eastern Alhambra opened in 1863, which stood close to the Olympia on the City side. Pitfield Street, Hoxton, is one of those down-at-heel, shabby old streets still to be found in these parts of London – a street of decayed eighteenth-century houses, cafés and mixed businesses. In the middle of the street, and alone worth the tour, is another once popular cheap music hall, Harwood's Varieties, a house run on the twice nightly system long before its general acceptance elsewhere and where salaries were paid on Sundays, when the theatre bars were open. Harwood's – or the Pitfield Varieties – is a pretty little theatre. It has four semi-circular arched windows, the dripstones of which end in clusters of carved leaves and flowers. These still bear traces of their original colour. The Royal arms (what member of Queen Victoria's family ever slipped off to Hoxton?) occupy the centre pilaster. Bearded men look down from the spandrils of the arches. All this part of the façade is mid-Victorian. Below is the entrance rebuilt in glazed terra-cotta, in that frigid Classic style of the 1914–1925 period used extensively in post offices and cinemas built soon after the Great War. In passing I might add that Pitfield Street has, in fact, an early cinema, now no longer used for its original purpose any more than is the music hall: a white stucco palace with a portico of green painted columns, left-overs of the English Renaissance. Harwood's Varieties was one of the many built as a theatre whose Victorian proprietors, finding music hall entertainments a more profitable venture, cut out Shakespeare and Sweeney Todd and realized on the potentialities of songs that reached the heart or occasioned a beery guffaw – songs of broken-hearted milkmen, of Empire occasions, of Jolly Jack Tar and Tommy Atkins, ballads of home, melancholy songs of unfortunates that started the unbidden tear, songs of Dixie, songs of London!

If you like to stare in the windows of Co-operative shops and old-fashioned drapers, if you have a fancy for cough drops and eel pies, Battersea is your Mecca. In York Road, Battersea, is (or was – the place is to come down and may have gone by the time this book is published) another interesting music hall, the Washington, whose most interesting period was when under the control of George Washington Moore, chief corner man and part owner of the Moore and Burgess Minstrels. The place dates from about 1886, and is of unique interest in view of its two pubs which formed the bars: the old Royal Standard was apparently already on part of the site and was incorporated in the theatre, another pub, the Washington, being added on the other side of the entrance. Both were used as theatre bars – they are still in use at the time of writing: two separate bars, each with its own name but with one landlord – a curiosity of licensing history. It was the first American-owned music hall in Britain. G. W. Moore was the father-in-law of Eugene Stratton, the famous coon delineator and original singer of 'The Lily of Laguna'; Stratton used to 'break in' all his new songs at his father-in-law's music hall. The Washington changed its name to the Battersea Palace about 1900. Evidently this failed to please, for in 1902 there was a further change, this time to the New Battersea Empire. Even so, perfection had not been achieved for the place became simply the Battersea Empire in 1906, after alterations. The final phase was complete modernization of the interior when it was transformed into the Super Palace Cinema in 1920. The two pub-bars of the Washington are somewhat dull affairs today, but the Washington bar contains a portion of a bar fitting in mahogany and engraved mirror glass. Not a vestige remains inside the music hall, which is nothing but an empty cavern with remnants of jazz decoration and leaded lights of 1920. Life was real, life was earnest in Battersea in the 'nineties. The Washington catered for local people, largely a coster population, whose market in Battersea High Street promised ample supplies of vegetable retribution for dud turns.

Other halls where chastisement was regularly handed out to ineffectual artistes were the Parthenon, Greenwich, and the Queen's, Poplar. The Queen's, once called the Apollo, remained tough to the last. 'Champagne Charlie' dragged out his last, illness-stricken week at the Queen's, keeping himself going on his favourite beverage and whelks.

I made a return journey to the Queen's quite recently, when checking on the notes made for this book. There had been so many changes in Poplar – great new blocks of flats and demolitions – that I hardly recognized the old High Street. The landlord of the local pub was a newcomer; a record player supplied the latest pop tunes. No one knew much about the Queen's, and I felt like Rip van Winkle. I found the music hall, however, and during my survey of its brokenhearted front, a cloth-capped ancient appeared. He at least remembered the Queen's and Marie Lloyd appearing there. Most of the façade is boarded up, but one of the original doorways with an especially fine coat-of-arms in the pediment remained intact. One of the doors swung open, and I picked my way over broken glass and lumber to the dark gallery. The interior had been much damaged, as might be expected, by hooligans. I remembered the rowdy audience which included such choice customers as decrepit old men, whose scent, whatever it was, was certainly not Chanel No. 5, and clownish youths. I recalled a woman breast-feeding her infant in her seat in the gods – the infant was a piccaninny, the mother white. The Queen's in its time did more than its share of lightening the dreary life of Poplar. Even the tough little chucker-out was an entertainment: I can still hear his curiously hoarse, plaintive cry in the interval, 'Cream hices! Luverly

TO
GALLERY
& CIRCLE

cream hices!' Then once more with considerable feeling, 'Won'tcher buy a cream-hice, guv?'

The songs and song covers are an inseparable part of the London halls. These song covers besides give lively insights into the London life of the Victorian period. Songs with titles like 'Costermonger Joe', 'We Girls at the Derby in a Four-in-Hand' or 'Doin' the Academy' gave rich opportunities for pictorial covers, designed as much with an eye to consumer appeal like the sleeve of a modern gramophone record as to decoratively illustrating the song. Of these covers, the best are those by Alfred Concanen, a Bohemian artist whose known work, almost entirely confined to song covers and book illustration, was little appreciated until recent years. Concanen has been compared (not very suitably) with Lautrec, for, needless to say, the Frenchman created a new and bitter art entirely peculiar to himself. Concanen was one of the several good illustrators of domestic subjects working in the 'sixties. If comparisons meant anything at all, he might more suitably be collated with Leech, though Concanen was a stronger draughtsman.

Concanen's 'Heavy Swell', based on Southern's character of Lord Dundreary, anticipates the best of du Maurier. The song cover of Leybourne as 'Champagne Charlie' shows the type to perfection; the light-hearted, whiskered masher, attired in clothes of a Mantalini-like charm, taps the champagne bottle with his cane, as if to demonstrate his settled policy of being the idol of the barmaids.

In other covers, the everyday incidents of Victorian street life in London – the flurry of omnibuses, of excursion trains, domestic squabbles and life in the second floor front, the humours of the zoo and the Royal Aquarium – are recorded. In many appear pleasing glimpses of London squares, bathed in a gentle sunshine. Concanen was at his best when recording the life of the London 'upper ten' – the follies of footmen, drawing-room simperings, cigar divans, the little annoyances that troubled even the dwellers in Belgravia. Or at least what was held to be the life of those flunkey-haunted regions, for the purposes of music hall consumption. Concanen's work as a book illustrator has music hall connections, for instance his vignettes to *The Carols of Cockayne* by Henry Leigh: these and the poems called *Strains from the Strand* were many of them set to music and became popular songs on the halls, especially 'The Shabby Genteel Man'. Leigh wrote extensively for *Punch*, and although his poetry – light verse would be a more accurate description – is by no means transcendent, there are many charming pieces in his disregarded volumes, verses possessing freshness and authenticity and at times a wistful quality. They may be compared with the paintings and drawings of Victorian London by minor or unknown artists that surprise and delight us in exhibitions, and they should certainly be read by connoisseurs of London. 'Over

Demolition of
Collins Music Hall, Islington

the Water' is a poem recalling the transpontine theatres of London and their
South Bank melodramas:

> Can I forget those wicked lords,
> Their voices and their calves;
> The things they did upon those boards,
> And never did by halves:
> The peasant, brave though lowly born,
> Who constantly defied
> Those wicked lords with utter scorn,
> Upon the Surrey side?

> But best of all I recollect
> That maiden in distress –
> So unimpeachably correct
> In morals and in dress –
> Who, ere the curtain fell, became
> The low-born peasant's bride:
> (They nearly always end the same
> Upon the Surrey side.)

There are other poems dealing with theatrical life – 'Treasury-Day' and 'A
Sigh from the Stalls'; yet another describes the chucker-out at the Gaiety
Restaurant in the Strand. Those who have an affection for the London of yesterday have a pleasure in store in these verses: I can recommend 'The Belle of the
Arcade', a fragrant, sentimental little piece on a doll seen in the Lowther Arcade,
a site now occupied by Coutts Bank. Before returning to the music halls, I cannot
resist quoting from a couple of poems that seem particularly felicitous. 'A
Cockney's Evening Song' conveys exactly a feeling of the City when the crowds
have gone:

> Temples of Mammon are voiceless again –
> Lonely policemen inherit Mark Lane
> Silent is Lothbury – quiet Cornhill –
> Babel of Commerce, thine echoes are still
> Far to the South – where the wanderer strays
> Lost among graveyards and riverward ways,
> Hardly a footfall and hardly a breath
> Comes to dispute Laurence-Pountney with Death.

And especially charming is 'Rotten Row':

> There's a tempting bit of greenery – of rus in urbe scenery –
> That's haunted by the London 'upper ten';

Caryatid of the
Metropolitan. May '68

Where, by exercise on horseback, an equestrian may force back
Little fits of tedium vitae now and then.

O! the times that I have been there, and the types that I have seen there
Of that gorgeous Cockney animal, the 'swell';
And the scores of pretty riders (both patricians and outsiders)
Are considerably more than I can tell.

When first the warmer weather brought these people all together,
And the crowds began to thicken through the Row,
I reclined against the railing on a sunny day, inhaling
All the spirits that the breezes could bestow.

That is all I think necessary to quote; you will see that the piece is pure Concanen.
Oddly, the artist did not illustrate it. 'Rotten Row' comes from *Carols of Cockayne*,
published by Chatto and Windus in 1874. Copies can be acquired cheaply
enough.

It is curious how the old music hall songs, often almost a-penny-a-line affairs,
knocked off at short notice, have preserved amid change and modification a whole
London world intact. Marie Lloyd's song about 'following the van' is an example;
latter-day attempts to provide a music hall bill find it indispensable, but only the
oldest Londoners can think of the thing as a piece of reporting: the midnight flit,
once so common, has become a thing of the past, like the shabby genteel man
and the amorous boy in the gallery. Again 'Every man of the Force has a watch
and chain of course' in the song 'If you want to know the time ask a policeman'
is an oblique reference to the widely held view that the police were not above
appropriating stolen watches to their own private use. 'Down the road away
went Polly' has given permanent expression to the rich coster life of the Old
Kent Road and the Cut, now all but obliterated, and George Lashwood's 'Riding
on top of a Car' recalls the upper deck courtships in the golden age of tram-
cars, when the hard seats and hissing wires proved no impediment to courtship.
Lurching and cumbersome it may have been, that tramcar of old time, but
spoony youths and maidens found it a car of dreams and its driver was named
'Romance'.

Today the surviving halls are either empty shells, bereft of furnishings, with as
little relation to the living theatre as a skeleton has to a living man, or like Wilton's
and Macdonald's turned to other uses; others have become cinemas or television
studios. It is but cold comfort to study the halls under these circumstances, but
the attempt should be made, particularly the later halls of the 'nineties when
fibrous plasterwork had reached its richest period. The decline began with the
new century: thenceforward theatre interiors in London showed an increasing

confusion of ideas, a distinct loss of panache, a less certain touch on the part of their architects.

Access to these abandoned theatres is often a matter of some difficulty. In a few instances exteriors are worth study – for example the Metropolitan and the Bedford – and one or two still have their attached public houses in use. It is incredible that these relics of a bygone London were not recorded photographically, one after the other, while still in use. I have done a certain amount myself by means of drawings, but a co-ordinated scheme would have had a unique value in the future. Such things are almost always left to chance, and a few cranks, in England. Only the Metropolitan, as far as I am aware, was photographed systematically. Nor is there much hope of a revival of music hall. When the remaining stars – Randolph Sutton, Billy Danvers and a few others – have dropped out, all connecting links will be severed. Most attempts at revival today are depressingly unlike the great periods: the gifted artistes of the calibre of Marie Lloyd are always inaccurately imitated, caricatured even: present-day talent cannot sustain a comparison with that of the past, new songs are a nightmare, audiences have had their ideas changed and their tastes debased. In a word, the music halls of London died from anaemia on one side of the footlights and bad nursing on the other. One might as well attempt to revive a corpse. So, if you have a feeling for London, study the music halls that remain. And, in order not to close on a depressing note, I end this chapter with a few extracts from the recollections of Emily Soldene, published when the halls were a vital part of life in town:

'The Oxford was a cosmopolitan place, and the audience also was cosmopolitan and various in its tastes and tendencies.

'The Hall, a magnificent structure in the Italian style, was beautifully decorated with frescoes, gilding and lots of light. Bars down the side were dressed with plenty of flowers, coloured glass and any amount of bright, glittering, brass-bound barrels and bottles. But, after all, the brightest, most glittering and most attractive thing about the bars (of course, not counting the drinks) were the barmaids. Rows of little tables, at which people sat and smoked and drank, filled the auditorium, and in and out the tables circulated the peripatetic, faded, suggesting, inquiring, deferential waiter, and the brisk, alert, "cigar", "programme" and "book of the words boy" . . . turning from these halls of dazzling light, one's mind turns back to those old times, and one cannot help wondering where the great respectable married music hallist and his "Missus" have migrated to. Do they gravitate to the East-end, or do they no longer exist? Perhaps they have passed away with "Vilikin's and his Dinah" and the "Ratcatcher's Daughter" or disappeared like the Days of Champagne Charley. . . .'

THREE

Bloomsbury:
Scenes that are Brightest

For me, for me, these old retreats
Across the world of London streets
My eye is pleased with all it meets
In Bloomsbury.

———————— * ————————

I LOVE BLOOMSBURY. I have done so since I lived there as a student. It was a glacial period – the Socialist winter of discontent, shortages, oppressions. None-theless (and although I have since relished them in less gruesome times), the qualities of Bloomsbury – the finest town architecture, great squares, curious and interesting people, old shops – went far to offset the lowering tendencies of those years. Indeed so perverse is the human mind – or at least mine is – that I can look back on some of the horrors of that time – for example, those dreadful British Restaurants – with a certain faint fondness. Those plates of grey mashed potatoes and horrid white beans, that bottle-green cabbage, the exhalations from which blended with those from the trousers of decaying old men, those beefy women whose heads were tied up like workmen's dinners, who slapped poultices of mash on thick, white plates! Eating at British Restaurants was cheap, students are always hungry and, anyway, those places put appetite to flight, thereby cutting costs to a minimum. After some preliminary trials, I selected the most dispiriting one to be found in Bloomsbury, a haven originally designed, about 1870, as a church hall. There was a dado round the walls, shoulder high, in that depressing colour I call 'Institution Brown'. Above the dado a cracked wall, painted in workhouse green, extended to the blackened ceiling. Beyond the serving hatch and vapours that joined with the breaths of diners and gases from old men to form a sort of permanent fog was a Gothic window of white and yellow glass. Above the window was a text in Lombardic capitals, 'Let everything that hath breath praise the Lord'. I thought this was wonderfully apt. You got extra value, too, for the prongs of the forks held fragments of previous dinners. Most of the old codgers had dew drops on the ends of their noses, like so many stalactites. You waited hopefully for the stalactites to descend among the hard faced beans, the bubble and squeak. They never did, for their owners sniffed them back at the crucial moment. Communal feeding centre, yclept Restaurant, I salute your memory, though your cottage pie was a hollow mockery and your semolina a thing of shame!

One of the most intriguing things about London is the way in which some districts have managed to preserve their identities within a metropolitan borough, or even, as with Bloomsbury, within two – Holborn and South St. Pancras. This is the more remarkable when the old village structure (such as Clerkenwell absorbed into Finsbury) is lacking. Still more interesting is the fact that Bloomsbury is itself subdivided into two compartments – the scholastic half north of Southampton Row and the more domestic one to the south. There are also minor subtler variations, such as the private enclave of Gray's Inn on the very edge of the district.

Euston Road defines one border of Bloomsbury. Start from St. Pancras church, a monument to the Greek revival, and infiltrate by way of Woburn Walk or one of the streets at right angles to Euston Road – where, by the way, besides the rich confectionery of St. Pancras Station, is a pretty little late Regency block, restored after the war to house homeless families and now empty, its cream stucco degenerated to a dirty yellow, and the cinema which was once the Euston Music Hall. Mabledon Place is a good point from which to plunge into the liveliest part of Bloomsbury. But first, go down Bidborough Street near the site of the Euston Market, a dull street once enlivened by the old stables topped by a benign red horse with a tail of unnatural length – all recently demolished. This leads to one of my favourite ports of call – the Salvation Army Supply Shop in Judd Street. The exterior remains exactly as when first built, with great red and gold signs on each side of the door, indicating the various departments within. You can buy tambourines and accordions here; transistor sets also, proving that the Army is not so old-fashioned as I like to believe; uniforms and devotional books; portraits of the Booth family, whiskery or with spectacles, and Salvation Army pencils. I regret that the superb Victorian texts, chromolithographed and entwined with flowers, seem to have disappeared; perhaps they were considered too period for present-day usage. A pity, for an illuminated 'God Bless our Home' would look good in the cabin of a space ship. Upstairs is an excellent restaurant, giving one the opportunity, as it might be, to sample a hot gospel and two veg.

While writing this chapter, I paid a return visit to my old studio in Cartwright Gardens, those dusty Elysian fields! This crescent is one of the handsomest among the second-class speculative architecture of Bloomsbury. The long windows of my rooms were still guarded by the iron bars placed there, I used to think, to discourage suicides. Overcome by sentiment, I thought of knocking on the door, but was it wise? A pretty girl appearing at the window decided me: it was unwise: I might weep on her shoulder. Cartwright Gardens has not changed much, at least along the crescent, since Johny Eames lived there under the auspices of Mrs. Roper. Burton Crescent (named after its builder) was its slightly more mundane title at the period of *The Small House at Allington*. Mrs. Roper was respectable, and would have disapproved of the tennis girls who come out with the spring to show various shapely portions of their anatomies and hint at others, while the blackbirds and thrushes make music in the plane trees.

Quite other music was made in my years there by a little weasel with a barrel organ, who played for the tarts and Canadian soldiers – all gone now, like last week's boarding house dinners. There was also a mournful cove with a cornet, very like the man in George Belcher's 'I dreamt I dwelt in marble halls'. On hot summer evenings when the Gardens were intolerably stuffy and airless and the sparrows too hot to squabble, the cornet player appeared at his window in shirt sleeves. He knew but one tune, 'Cruising down the River', and was apt to become tedious after the first hour or so.

A few hotels remain in the crescent – Jenkin's Hotel, the Crescent, the Mentone and so on. I have often wondered what it was in the climate of Bloomsbury that attracted the boarding houses and temperance hotels. The boarding houses associated with that stage of my career will long remain in memory. One day I may combine them into a composite picture of Bloomsbury life, crummy, unbelievable, almost extinct. The Misses Ponsonby's was a frowning fastness of utter respectability. Endless flights of stairs led from the dark entrance hall to the little back room I had in the roof – a sky-parlour behind the parapet. There was always a smell on the landing – the mixed odours of sixty years of London dinners having ascended to the house top, impregnating the very wallpaper. Half of my room was unusable because of its sloping ceiling. The other half would have accommodated an average-sized Alsatian, if he had short legs. An alcove in part of the room was mysteriously screened from view, behind a crazy washstand, by a sort of curtain. One day, my curiosity could stand it no longer: I had to see behind the veil. I might have found the mummified figure of a long dead lodger. What I did find was a collection of chamber pots – about forty of them – mainly floral. One surprisingly had an engraving of a Congregational church. Besides the jerries were a number of photographs in Oxford frames of soldiers of the Great War. Stranger things awaited me that morning, however, for when I emerged from the recess, I found that the skivvy, a prematurely aged little oddity, angular and red-eyed, had entered the room. She suddenly leaped on the bed, pulled down a pair of grubby drawers and said, quite unjustifiably, 'This is what you've

always wanted.' The indescribable quality of the situation struck me forcibly –
the shrivelled, pathetic creature on the bed and myself standing there, covered
with dust, holding out a chamber pot decorated with a view of a Congregational
church. . . . Sickert changed to Rowlandson in the twinkling of an eye. Time and
change have overtaken the Misses Ponsonby's. Today not so much as a doorplate
remains of the gloomy house that formed a reservoir for those brackish, unquiet
waters of the moon.

Marchmont Street, the shopping street of this part of Bloomsbury, is still of
interest, though its character is going. The old post office has vanished. London
post offices of the little streets would make an unusual London excursion;
delightful ones remain in Lisson Grove and Stoke Newington Church Street.
The Edwardian grocer's has gone, too, but a pretty butcher's can still be seen, a
shop with gracefully engraved glass, pots of fern and pigs' heads with apples in
the mouth.

Bloomsbury was one of the earliest residential areas of London, and though
its fine domestic architecture and spacial qualities have suffered from the intru-
sion of out-of-scale blocks such as the Senate House of London University,
utterly out of sympathy with the Bloomsbury terraces and squares, something of
the old refined character can be seen even yet. That character owes much to the
Bloomsbury squares, the important ones being in the academic territory north of
Southampton Row. Bloomsbury Square, laid out as early as the seventeenth
century – though its original houses have all disappeared (the gardens were
planted out by Repton about 1800), Woburn Square, Gordon Square, Tavistock
Square and Russell Square, the last illustrated on page 43, are the most remarkable. During my Bloomsbury days, the last two were pretty rough, the gardens
suffering from the neglect of the war years. At night they were alive with soldiers
and girls; it was impossible to walk a few yards without stumbling over them.
Their noises off floated from the undergrowth. Bloomsbury squares had become
the fields of Venus and Mars.

Now the Holborn Council have made them delightful again: children and
dogs, lawns and flowerbeds, tea-houses and playgrounds have taken over and
Venusberg is no more. Russell Square, also laid out by Repton, has had its
terraces spoiled by later Victorian tinkering, but I am very attached to the
Hotels Russell and Imperial, particularly when seen through the leaves of the
plane trees. Both are by the same architect, Fitzroy Doll. Sitting on the benches
of the square in the evening light, you can imagine yourself as the owner of a
great and ancient park and chateau, the turrets of which shine through the trees,
the strollers in the square, being, of course, the public whom you have charitably
let in for nothing. Most critics of architecture deplore these examples of the terra-
cotta age. However, I love their magnificent scenic effects, especially the Imperial

– cheerful mongrel of *art nouveau*/Belgian Gothic. I like its mosaic sundial and Turkish baths and the statues of King Edward VII and Queen Alexandra. These statues are in Gothicky niches that also accommodate cheeky Bloomsbury pigeons, whose droppings have plastered the waistcoat of good King Edward and the bosom of Queen Alexandra. The Russell is more restrained; admire the Cupid lamps placed at intervals along the front. The recently built porch is a mistake, and should be ignored for it is painfully out of harmony with the original work. The other two statues on the Imperial are also amusing – Julius Caesar and Charlemagne. Imperially minded these two may have been, but their connection with the splendours and miseries of hotel life is obscure: still, the imperturbable pigeons treat them all alike.

These Bloomsbury squares, notably Bedford Square, are London's distinctive contribution to the art of living in town, restrained, rational, altogether civilized. Nothing better has been devised, nor ever will be. The shapes and sizes of the squares vary, and this, together with the pattern made by alternate squares and terraces, prevents dullness and monotony. In addition, the various terrace blocks vary in treatment of detail. Fortunately, Bedford Square, c. 1775, is to be preserved intact. It is without question the finest square in London, and a source of never failing pleasure when one has traversed the gloomy length of Gower Street. Not that I would have Gower Street altered – the new buildings at the Euston Road end have already done sufficient damage to it – but it is a little uninspiring. The Bedford Square end of Gower Street has a connection with nineteenth-century English art, for the Millais family lived there, and talks between the young Royal Academy prizewinner and his friend Holman Hunt led to the founding of the Pre-Raphaelite Brotherhood – oddly unimaginative surroundings for a movement that was to produce so much strangeness and passion.

One of the joys of Gower Street when I was at the Slade was the famous antique shop, Simmonds, on the Euston Road corner. In those days, the firm regularly displayed pictures, frames and engravings on the pavement, often in quantity. Size and colour seemed to be the criterion in determining prices: there was always the unexpected thrill of the chase. I shall never forget my chagrin when, one memorable Thursday morning, I decided against my usual inspection. The pictures had not changed for a fortnight – finds, therefore, seemed at a discount. Professor Schwabe looked in on his way from Hampstead, and found a Rossetti drawing which he bought for sixteen shillings. . . . Even then, I had not fully learned from experience, for I later bought a nineteenth-century landscape. This I thought was by George Richmond, the portrait painter. A good guess, certainly, though not good enough, for I parted with it before finding it to be by Lear. Until recently, across the Euston Road were those little Italian cafés,

where we used to consume Vienna steaks (we will remember Vienna steaks) and chips with everything.

Today the private houses in the University area are fast disappearing, routed by students' Halls of Residence, clubs, social centres and whatnot. The intellectuals of the Fry-Woolf kind who lived in them are seen no more; perhaps it is as well. The new intellectual life of Bloomsbury has a purely utilitarian end: it gets its degree, returns to the provinces or to what was once the Empire, and teaches happily ever after. At no time an intellectual myself, and detesting art discussion above all things, I nevertheless felt it right to buy the painting by Roger Fry I found screening a broken hole in a Bloomsbury bathroom . . . it only cost me two shillings.

The squares of South Bloomsbury are of less moment. One of the great losses to the area was the demolition of the Foundling Hospital with its pictures by Hogarth and curious chapel where Handel played on the organ, turning it into a fashionable rendezvous and so augmenting the charity's finances. Of the early nineteenth-century (c. 1820) Regent Square, only one side is intact. The rest was bombed and has been replaced by slabs of flats. But the surviving terrace adjoining the Scottish Church (mentioned in Chapter 7) has shapely iron balconies of the old Bloomsbury pattern. These balconies, when the sunlight is at the right angle, cast interesting diagonal shadows on the dull stucco of the ground floor. One part of the terrace projects, displaying on its end wall the faded announcement

ANTURIO BATH SALTS
Cure Gout and Rheumatism
BATES'S SALVE
Cures Wounds and Sores.

The bombed church of St. Peter (1824–6, Greek Revival, like St. Pancras and also by Inwood, but of a cut-price character) remains, or at least the portico and circular tower, shadowed by plane trees. The rest of the church is an empty shell. In front, the blackbirds and thrushes sing on a summer evening and pigeons strut among geraniums and gasping old men. The old men found in this part of Bloomsbury differ from those encountered in the humanist area. Round the British Museum, they are projections from Gissing, shabby, scholarly, given to carrying shapeless brown paper parcels. The Reading Room is their club, where their trembling fingers turn the pages of obscure reference books. Sometimes they furtively nibble a crust. You never see them anywhere but in the museum area. Their eyes are watery and their gaze, fixed on the past, is entirely lacking in hope. They are, in fact, Henry Ryecrofts.

Judd Street leads into Brunswick Square, the former qualities of which – dull, perhaps, but reasonable – are now mostly shorn away. Here again, blocks of student accommodation and similar intruders are taking the place of the terraced houses. The house where Ruskin was born survives, a private hotel offering H & C in all rooms. Round the corner, towards the fringe of the district and best approached from Guildford Place, is my favourite Bloomsbury pub, the Lamb, possessing one of the finest Victorian interiors in London. Comfortable padded and buttoned settees line the wall along one side, blending to perfection with the brass-railed, cast-iron tables, the legs of which are ornamented with figures of Britannia. Above are rows of photographs of Victorian and Edwardian stage celebrities, faded but choice, and eighteenth-century engravings, including one of the benevolent Captain Coram. A gas bracket with a pink glass shade is a fit companion for the musical comedy beauties. A few steps down from the bar lead to a sort of private snuggery, where the walls are hung with embossed paper in an *art nouveau* pattern. The pub ceiling is supported by iron columns having palm branch capitals, an Egyptian device taken over on some few occasions by the Greeks and later to become a basic item in the extensive repertoire of the nineteenth-century pub architect. The mahogany bar of the Lamb is a reassuring example of Victorian design and craftsmanship, all solid stuff. There are turned columns and a row of splendid hinged windows, engraved with 'brilliant' stars, to separate the view of the masses from the gaze of the classes. On the bar counter is a penny-in-the-slot musical box, the kind with a revolving disc of steel which appeared just before the general popularity of the phonograph. The Lamb's character has been carefully preserved by the present owners. The whole thing is a collector's piece with solid and liquid refreshment to match.

From here, Great Ormond Street, with its early eighteenth-century doors, leads to Queen Square, an interesting place of mixed architectural styles. The area contains a number of hospital buildings dating from the 1870's onwards. One might write a book on the workhouse, asylum and hospital architecture of London. The Italian Hospital in Queen Square, built in 1899 by Cutler, has an oddly Continental air; next to it are the fine Georgian houses of the Stanhope Institute. Gothic is represented by St. George's School, by S. S. Teulon, an architect whose work nearly always leaves an uncomfortable, gloomy impression on the mind. Admirers of nineteenth-century cast iron (all the readers of this book, I hope) have a select item here – the stumpy, Elizabethan style fountain, on which details of sixteenth-century strapwork decoration are reproduced in metal. It is very pretty and topped by a Victorian lamp.

But the Victorians outraged the neighbouring church of St. George-the-Martyr. Only they, surely, could be so unfeeling as to take an eighteenth-century church (1706) and then trick it out with incongruous Romanesque details. Obviously the church was considered dowdy and unfashionable architecturally when these improvements were made in 1867–8. To Gothicize it was, perhaps, too tall an order; luckily the Romanesque style came in handy as second best. So a great fat porch was clapped on, an ugly customer, and the eighteenth-century windows filled with dismal Romanesque tracery of the sort which, with a similar audacity, transmogrified Wren's church of St. Mary Aldermanbury. Other incongruous details were added inside, notably the Byzantine-like reredos and the window above. In spite of all this the interior still has the general arrangement of an eighteenth-century preaching church. There is a plaster ceiling of simple character supported on Corinthian columns. The roof has an odd Gothic spire, not the least of the eccentricities of St. George's.

The British Museum cannot be given more than a short amount of space in a book on off-beat London, obviously. There is, however, a curious experience to be had there on Sundays, for the crowds awaiting admission beguile their time (and very sensibly, too) by looking in the windows of the conjuring shop opposite, 'a dealer in magic and spells'. It is a charming shop in rich, late Victorian premises, and can be brought into one view with the stately museum across the street. Here you may purchase all kinds of magic equipment and toilet rolls with encouraging messages specially printed on them. It is a disappointing fact that no traces exist today of magic shops of the sinister kind described in the short story by H. G. Wells: but there are shops dealing in occult literature here. At one of them, I once found an ancient treatise on raising the Devil and sundry other infernal creatures. It was an intriguing book, so I felt sure that, if I bought it, I should be tempted to try it out. As, like Oscar Wilde, I can resist anything except temptation, it seemed better not to become the owner.

Museum Street and its tributaries offer much to the lover of old books. The fine Victorian pub full of stained and coloured glass, the Museum Tavern, is a choice place for students of the subject: it belongs to the transitional period between the gin palace and the full-blown pub of the 1890's, of which the Salisbury in St. Martin's Lane is probably the finest example. Here, too, was Meatyard's, surely one of the most agreeable shops ever found in London, devoted to the sale of old drawings and watercolours; next door was another shop of a curiously macabre interest, selling artificial limbs. The two shops and the pub provided an agreeable way of spending a Bloomsbury morning: to feast on the drawings until the mind was incapable of more, then a quarter of an hour gazing at the legs and arms next door and the whole rounded off by a couple of glasses of stout in the taproom of the pub, where the floor was sanded and the benches scrubbed and the pretence that one was a Victorian navvy easily accomplished.

I rarely pass the front of the British Museum without thinking of the Rossetti poem, 'The Burden of Nineveh', the publication of which did so much to

augment the poet's Oxford circle. In fact, I often go in simply to stare at those dreadful creatures from Babylon and Nineveh. For those winged bulls and man-headed lions never fail to inspire awe and an uncomfortably acute sense of the infinite wastage of years. Those frightful beasts were staring like that when Jesus Christ was born – ages before, for that matter – and have been staring so ever since. The marks of the sculptor's chisel are as fresh as if made yesterday. Similar thoughts occur in the rooms devoted to Egyptian antiquities, especially the more personal objects – mirrors, paintboxes, toys: all have the same power to call up disagreeable reflections, terrible feelings of transience and change. But the museum authorities have done the only thing possible to alleviate such desolate imaginings by stationing stolid, sensible attendants in peaked caps, and these characters, though by no means a cure, are a distinct relief, especially when they give expression to their private views, as I heard one do on a sweltering hot day: 'Fancy being cooped up with these bloody mummies on a day like this!'

Among the Greek and Roman collections, there is a part of an inscription to a Roman Governor of Britain, found on Tower Hill. Most people pass it without knowing its unique history, though it is of special interest to Londoners. This inscription, erected by the Governor's wife, formed part of a memorial to her husband. It is London's only direct contact with the New Testament, for these two Romans knew Pontius Pilate. As a tailpiece to the museum, take a look at the statue from Easter Island presented to Queen Victoria, and pity the Royal Family, a sitting target for all the crackpot, inconceivable presents it is possible to muster.

Although James Smith's in New Oxford Street on the edge of Bloomsbury more properly belongs to the chapter on shops, I cannot resist including it here and the drawing of it is opposite. The premises are Victorian Renaissance above, with Gothic ironwork below on the fascia. Such shops were once abundant in London, and are now a rarity. Smith's is an absolutely perfect late Victorian shop, complete in every detail, and ought to be protected under the Town and Country Planning Act. The owners must be unusually enlightened, for I cannot imagine why the place has not been ruined long ago. Only the now demolished offices of *Truth* (gloriously 1870, with carved wood, stained glass and leather) could give so much intense satisfaction. Smith's is remarkable for its lavish display of that ornamental lettering so appealing to Victorians of any period. There is a device of a White Ensign and star-spangled banner above the door and the legend 'English and American Umbrella and Stick Stores'. An engraved brass plate runs round the base of the windows and below that a glass-faced plinth, lettered in black, red and gold – the capital letters are ornamented with a flower decoration, tradescantia apparently. The whole thing glitters with brass and gold leaf, and the cast iron outer door is good enough to be a part of the Coalbrookdale Gate. It was the custom in the late nineteenth century to take every opportunity to detail your

Bloomsbury Umbrella Shop
with Budington Bertie.

wares on shop fronts; other announcements, therefore, offer Riding Crops and Whips, Irish Blackthorns and Malacca Canes; also, reminiscent of an earlier, less settled period in London when a man might be called upon to defend himself at any moment (the period of Corinthian Tom and Jerry), Dagger Canes, Life Preservers and Sword Sticks. Smith's door has those white porcelain letters of old time: similar ones advertising Fry's and Cadbury's chocolate can still be found on the windows of ancient sweet shops. This is the only part of New Oxford Street where a Victorian atmosphere can be recaptured. There is a frilly bracket clock opposite Smith's and a drinking fountain of marble a few yards away. Behind Smith's shop is the Bloomsbury Baptist Church, a study in nineteenth-century Romanesque, gaunt, black and white and severe of aspect. As I made the accompanying drawing, a down-and-out with an ineffable air of jaunty hopelessness hove into view – Burlington Bertie himself, without a doubt, toddling up West.

Another border of Bloomsbury runs along Tottenham Court Road from Great Russell Street. A few old houses of the seventeenth and eighteenth centuries still remain, notably No. 99, Great Russell Street, with a great, wide staircase and a painting in the manner of Verrio on the ceiling above (illustrated on page 47). No doubt, all these old houses will eventually disappear.

There is nothing much to detain one in Tottenham Court Road, except Lyon's Corner House (on the site previously mentioned of the Oxford Music Hall) and the Rising Sun, a pub in the Gothicky, *art nouveau* style of 1897, though there is an establishment in this area – I need not be more exact – where one can acquire those dreary-choice strip-tease films, shown in the Soho joints to amuse patrons before the live show commences. Maison Dietrich, the 1910 vintage hairdressers for women, has only recently disappeared: the shop was a gem of *art nouveau* decoration, and right up to the end, the window displayed waxen heads of an Edwardian type of beauty – the kind represented by Phyllis Dare and Edna May. Mortimer Market, a humble but entirely delightful little square, occupied in the centre by a block of terraced cottages and shop fronts of the early nineteenth century, has also gone, never restored after war damage. One might have passed the narrow entrance in Tottenham Court Road many times, unaware of the charming little 'market' behind, where old men stood to gossip under the gas lamps. Shepherd Market in Mayfair is a slightly larger, flashier and self-conscious version.

Two more items in the Bloomsbury itinerary remain to be mentioned – St. George's, Bloomsbury, and Red Lion Square, or what remains of it. Hawksmoor's architecture is always remarkable for grandiose scenic qualities, in association with a certain penchant for oddity shared, as far as I know, by no other English architect apart from Butterfield, the Gothic Revivalist. St. George's is very theatrical in its interior arrangements. Nothing in Bloomsbury is grander than its deep portico and nothing odder than the stepped pyramidal spire, based on the Mausoleum of Halicarnassus, and topped by a statue of King George I.

Red Lion Square was much damaged in the War, when its Gothic Revival church of St. John, by Pearson, was ruined. The new roadway into Holborn has since sliced away one side of the square and new blocks have altered its former character almost out of recognition. I remember it as a dark, reserved old square, with a poor little fountain playing almost to itself. Fortunately, the house where Morris and Burne-Jones set up a studio together remains. Visit it and the rest of Bloomsbury in the fall of the year when the autumn fires are lit in the squares, and mourn the decay of London.

FOUR

London Villages

——— * ———

APART FROM a house in Cheyne Walk or chambers in Albany, I can think of no greater earthly felicity than owning one of the Georgian houses in Hampstead. Sickert once said that his idea of Heaven was that it resembled the Caledonian Market; there is much to be said for the notion, but Hampstead – its increasing traffic and new flats excepted – seems an even better comparison. One is compelled to admit that its allegedly high rate of suicide is, if true, at variance with the idea of Hampstead's being an earthly paradise: but even Heaven had its dissatisfied ones, if Satan began business as a fallen angel. Authors on London often like to describe it as a collection of villages; a very far-fetched conception in reality, for over the whole of London nearly all local character has been obliterated, largely by the agency of an overall system of government, calculated to subdue all individuality into a common mediocrity. Londoners, themselves, have undergone a like processing and are now only too ready to conform to an average type, with all idiosyncrasies painlessly removed.

Even so, there are enough remnants of the one-time London villages and small communities to be found in various parts of London to deserve a short review, especially as the days of all local character are numbered. Hampstead, which I hope will resist change and erosion to the last, is, of all the London rural retreats, the one retaining most of its eighteenth-century charm. Indeed, two of its own hamlets, North End and The Vale of Health, still have hints of their former independence. It is well for Hampstead that so much was done there in the eighteenth century, both the small terraces and the larger houses – a development aided by its popularity as a London spa – before the mid-Victorians moved in, grimly, from Chalk Farm and Finchley. There are certain Victorian buildings in Hampstead which I greatly admire, but not many: here the Victorians (apart from those who fought to preserve the Heath) and the Edwardians did much damage. As if this ugliness were not enough, there are other modern schemes constantly threatening Hampstead – horrors which, if carried out, will ruin it alike for those who live there and those who visit it. A wall like the great wall of China ought to be built round Hampstead and only those able to prove them-

selves fit ought to be allowed in. Car door bangers would be excluded of neces-
sity; armed vigilantes would pick off jeenagers and rowdies on sight from
the walls. Hitherto, Hampstead has resisted attempts to turn it into a third-rate
Montmartre. Such changes would be alien, and especially wrong at night when
the village is dark and mysterious. Dusk, when the lamps are lighted in the little
squares, gives Hampstead an effect altogether charming – the dusk that envelopes
its old garden walls and lime-shaded passages and alleys in velvety darks and
triangular shadows – Passy at night in the time of Balzac must have been similarly
delightful, or so I like to think.

When I used to visit Gladys Joseph, Holman Hunt's daughter, in her great
house in Akenside Road, coming away full of tea, cake and Pre-Raphaelitism, I
would wander up Heath Street and think of that wonderful artist, Ford Madox
Brown, painting the background to his picture called 'Work' and the landscape,
never to be forgotten, that he also painted in Hampstead, 'English Autumn
Afternoon' – boy and girl lovers in the foreground, tints of the falling year in a
glowing distance beyond.

It is pleasant to imagine Hampstead in its fashionable time as a spa, when
those Londoners who could afford it took a coach out of the crowded city to take
the waters, or to attend the races on the Heath or to idle in Well Walk and Church
Row, the fashionable promenades of the little town; when Hampstead in the days
of Addison exported its waters, bottled in Flask Walk, to various parts of London;
or at a later period, before the Underground came, when Mr. du Maurier was at
work on *Trilby*. Today, a Bank Holiday on Hampstead Heath is a mere shadow
of its former self: the crowds are not the same – they have forgotten how to enjoy
themselves as their Cockney ancestors did on those rare days out of long ago –
but the swings, gaily painted and carved, are graceful and pretty through the
trees. Occasionally the steam yachts appear or a roundabout of the 'nineties, and
the helter-skelter still offers its unsophisticated thrills. But the crowds are un-
receptive. So much so that, on one of my visits, I heard a Londoner, in the pitch
black interior of a ghost show, complain that Hampstead had no thrills to offer
and no excitement. I reached across in the dark in order to oblige him, and stuck
my iced lolly down his neck.

Time was when things were different on a Hampstead Bank Holiday. Before
me as I write is a large drawing by Phil May in which all the life, vulgarity and
cheerful spirit of this coster carnival has been concentrated. A group of coster
girls dance a kind of Palais Glide to the music of an accordion. In the foreground,
a screaming kid, lost, no doubt, holds up a balloon. Crowds sit out on the grass
behind, decked in holiday finery – flowing hats, check suits, titfers; a coster gives
his Donah a whacking kiss, which she returns with interest in the shape of a
thick ear; hot tea is a penny, bread and butter likewise.

This period was a great one for the Old Bull and Bush, now rebuilt and with relics of Florrie Forde, who sang its praises and those of the German band in the tea gardens behind. The pub, pretty in those days before the Great War, had two bay windows, snug and inviting, on each side of the door and window boxes and tubs. Cockneys, in the long skirts of the period, in boaters, tight boots and Eton collars, came on Sunday mornings for the 2s. Ordinary, served from two to three o'clock. Such a crowd has assembled in front of the Bull and Bush in one of several old photographs I have of it: a young man in a boater looks inquiringly at a pretty girl in skirt and blouse, carrying a reticule on her arm; a gent with a walrus moustache, attended by a collie dog, is obviously arguing with a coster acquaintance who makes his point with the stem of the clay pipe he is about to light. Similar scenes took place at many of the old village pubs of London, especially, as I have said, at the Old Welsh Harp:

> Me in my pearlies felt a toff that day
> Down at the Welsh 'Arp which is 'Endon way.

One of the pleasures of Hampstead is the panorama of London from the Heath at Spaniards Walk. Years ago, on a clear day, it was possible to see as far as Box Hill in Surrey. Now the prospect offers a startling view of the changes taking place in the shape of London. Older developments are confined to a horizontal plane, for the new London skyline is climbing vertically, a Cockney Manhattan. From Hampstead, however, its harshness is softened by a foreground of hornbeams and thickets where the brambles grow and by the pools left in the sandy hollows. Sand was regularly dug from the Heath in the Victorian period, and carted to London for sanding the floors of taverns and alehouses. In winter, the scene is enlivened by the flocks of starlings (true connoisseurs of London) who divide their time between the Heath and the West End.

> See where lovely Hampstead stands
> And the wond'ring Vale commands
> What surprising prospects rising
> All around adorn ye lands.

Yes, there is much to be said for the Northern delights of Hampstead . . . Happy Hampstead, where little squares and dolls' houses soothe the vexed spirit of the Londoner; full of memories of Constable, Kate Greenaway and du Maurier; offering many pleasantnesses to the eye; where duffle-coated figures sell *Peace News* at the Underground and where even a modern Bank Holiday man can enjoy himself in a lachrymose way, leaving behind him a trail of souvenirs on the grass – milk cartons, fag packets and contraceptives!

I recently walked the whole way to Camberwell in order to appreciate what the lower orders in the City had to endure before public transport arrived, or after that if they were impecunious. To tramp this distance, as so many did, twice daily in all weathers was no mean undertaking. Camberwell, with its ad-joining villages of Dulwich and Peckham Rye, remained rural until the 1830's, when the building mania overtook it, but areas of open land remained in places as late as the 1870's. One can imagine the mortification of sensitive Victorians, such as Ruskin, who witnessed this wholesale destruction of the pasture land and the market and strawberry gardens by the speculative builders. Even now the process is not complete, for Camberwell and Brixton have taken an immense influx of coloured immigrants, and a new and not altogether attractive pattern has emerged. One may hazard a guess that Brixton will eventually be emptied of its original inhabitants, who, in moving out, are giving up the district to the new-comers. Soon only negroes and policemen will be left.

Going from London in the direction of Camberwell, one leaves the new nightmare landscape of the Elephant behind without regret. It is hard to decide which is the more deplorable – the clutter of worn-out rubbish formerly occupy-ing the site or the dehumanized, oppressive blocks which have taken its place. However, things improve when you are once past the railway arch and into Wal-worth Road with an encouraging start in the shape of a splendid herbalist's, Baldwins, described in the next chapter. The whole of the route, one of the earliest urban developments in Camberwell, is lined with radio shops, cheap dress shops, jewellers, built out in front of the early nineteenth-century terraces. Along the Walworth Road, adjoining the Temple Bar Wine Lodge, is an old-fashioned shop of a kind becoming increasingly rare. This is L. J. Hopton's wool shop, established 1852. The building is late eighteenth-century brick with creamwashed walls and pantiled roof and picturesque low windows divided by substantial glazing bars. Steps go down to the shop, the floor of which is now below pavement level.

Two street markets here are worth exploring for the barrow life of Walworth – East Street and Westmorland Road. The latter has one of the few modern jellied eel shops. There is another not quite so streamlined on Walworth Road with the neon-lit notice 'Jellied Eels. No Waiting' as if to imply that, once the notion of jellied eels has entered the Cockney head, it is unwise for him to delay carrying the idea into action. There is also a richly traditional jellied eel shop almost opposite Westmorland Road, displaying the mirrors essential to a well-con-ducted establishment and green and yellow tiles: the building dates from the mid-1870's. Walworth Road has fragmentary remains of its old architecture right up to Camberwell Green in severe Bloomsbury-type houses with iron balconies. Many are decayed and nearly all turned over to industrial purposes; a few have been carefully restored for use as offices. Some still remain in private occupation, with patches of rough grass representing a lawn, plane trees, dustbins and work-ing-class cats. Photographs of fat infants, hand tinted to a porky pink, fill the photographers' windows, and the infants themselves fill the prams parked outside self-service stores, goggling at jumbo-sized packets of soap powder.

Camberwell Green (the original title of Mendelssohn's 'Spring Song' com-posed in Camberwell in 1842) was once surrounded by fine old houses, no traces of which now remain. Camberwell Fair, a three-day event almost rivalling that at Greenwich, was held on the Green, offering, as late as the 1840's, enter-tainments such as barnstorming melodramas, a travelling pub and collections of curiosities which at that period included a mermaid who played a harp. Mer-maids have vanished from the Green, like the butterfly named after its old habitat, the Camberwell Beauty. Today the place is visited mainly by old men, mostly asleep on the green-painted forms or else staring vacantly at the circling buses. Dogs sniff at each other's behinds, while the pigeons try a little late-season courting; the chestnut and plane leaves are blown along in the thin November air and the last roses of the Camberwell summer wither against a background of Peabody flats. Here is one of the finest lavatories in London, albeit a little worse for long and rough usage. A double staircase of cast iron, painted green, termin-ates below in ornamental newel posts. There is a black and white floor, and the place is fitted with pink marble stalls, rather eroded. Its most unusual feature is the circular, mahogany wash place in the centre, with engraved glass windows. Gas lighting gives an essential finishing touch.

Camberwell Church Street has fascinating shops: a health and strength establishment, displaying pictures of muscular men and women, and the Govern-ment Surplus Store, selling genuine army cooks' trousers, genuine pullovers, genuine socks and second-hand clothing, including an assortment of spike helmets and solar topees. Best of all, they still favour the old-fashioned, waxen-headed dummies. These dummies have entirely disappeared from the windows of tailoring concerns, with a corresponding loss of interest. I was enthusiastic for those pale-faced manikins with real hair and staring glass eyes. And I know but one shop left in the whole of London where they still have male and female fashion plates of the 1920's on show, and this only because the proprietors have forgotten to change the window since the General Strike.

St. Giles Parish Church in Camberwell Church Street is by Sir Gilbert Scott in collaboration with Moffatt, his early partner in the designing of workhouses. It is big, adequate, without vitality or conviction, with a machine-made look about it. The old parish church, near the foot of The Grove was destroyed by fire in 1841, the present building of Kentish rag being consecrated by the end of 1844. The tall spire is the important feature, yet on a close inspection the handling of the details is raw and unappealing. Scott had not yet developed into the

LIFE WITH THE
WINDMILL GIRLS

SENIOR
SERVICE
Satisfy

R WHITES

RACING

MILK

TIZER
THE
APPETIZER

W
Wells

The Grove Camberwell

competent universal provider of Gothic, though the commonplace nature of
Scott's later work is very pronounced. The use of Kentish rag became a formula
for Gothic churches as the century progressed, often in areas quite unsuitable for
its use. St. Giles was much admired at the time of its erection, though Eastlake
comments on the unworthiness of the wood fittings and the coarseness of decorative carving in the capitals, which, he says, are better in design than execution.
The white distempered interior and the dullness of Scott's furnishings do not
help matters, and the east window, in the design of which Ruskin and Edmund
Oldfield took a hand, has all the purplish blue and red rawness characteristic of
the stained glass of the period. There is a wooden model of the church under a
single light Good Samaritan window; the porch at the rear is hideously scored
with dates and initials, very mournful. The graveyard has one or two interesting
old tombs and graves, including that of the cantankerous wife of John Wesley.

Camberwell Grove, illustrated on the previous page, is surprisingly rural. Its
Georgian houses of mellowed yellow-grey brick have a character quite unlike the
rest of the district. Camberwell was built up in the nineteenth century by many
small builders in two main periods roughly coinciding with the coming of the rail-
ways – a somewhat late arrival – and the later era of the horse tram. Fortunately,
The Grove was almost complete by the 1840's, and presented an agreeable com-
pound of late eighteenth-century terraced houses and semi-detached villas rising
to the top of the hill. It was a place of residence for the gentry and quality of the
neighbourhood, and has remained virtually intact ever since. Tea gardens and an
assembly room made their appearance at one time, patronized by those would-be
fashionables who appear so frequently in the Sketches by Boz. Tall and delicate
trees rustle graceful foliage, shadowing the fronts of the old houses and diminish-
ing uphill in a green perspective: one is reminded of Hobbema's picture of the
Avenue at Middleharnis. Pregnant women, drearily resigned to their fate of
pushing prams, appear and disappear in the pools of golden light moving across
the pavement. Tottering, ancient, old girls make the ascent by easy stages. The
Grove is awaiting a return to fashion. A few of the detached villas are very typical
of those spruce residences ('neat' was the usual adjective) favoured by traders and
merchants at the Boz period – Nos. 36 and 34, for example, which retain their
lace curtains and dark varnished doors, and on the opposite side farther up, an
attractive, three-storied villa with cream-painted stucco front, portico of Ionic
columns and a shallow arched fanlight over the Regency-type door, the whole
thing preserving its period flavour so completely that your imagination has no
trouble in seeing the City man in stove-pipe hat bowl up to the garden gate in gig
or carriage, armed with a copy of Mr. Dickens's latest number.

Unlike many villages on the once rural edges of London, Strand-on-the-
Green, a strip of old houses, inns and wharves on the river facing the Surrey

side, has remained almost unaltered, apart from a small group of contemporary houses on Magnolia Wharf, since the eighteenth century. In order to obtain the value of sharp contrast, approach it by rail. Gunnersbury Station would, I believe, receive a gold medal in any contest for the most depressing station in Greater London. Inner London would have Wapping, which, besides melancholy, possesses drama: Gunnersbury is dreariness itself ('Some cry up Gunnersbury, for Sion some declare'). The station's air of desolation is a suitable beginning for the deadly walk to Strand-on-the-Green: under the concrete railway arch where the shattered gas lamps are, and empty whisky bottles half-buried in cinder, where the Japanese knot-weed, most sinister of railway-loving plants, grows rank and lurid on the spare ground. Next come the 1930-ish flats of Chiswick village, and before the river is reached, those dreadful streets of Victorian, terraced houses built of ferocious red brick (belonging spiritually to the suburbs of Manchester) where once stood orchards and riverside pleasaunces.

But Strand-on-the-Green, with its delightful, old houses, narrow ways and willows weeping in the river, is ample compensation. There are comfortable riverside pubs here, especially satisfying to patronize when the day is hot. All are good but my favourite is the Bull's Head, this being a shade more old-fashioned than the others. From its window seats, one can enjoy the views of the river through a foreground of geraniums. There the sun sparkles on the moving water from a bright sky, lightly flecked with little clouds: the train crossing the railway bridge at once recalls some picture by Monet. Chestnuts are in bloom across the river, and on the eighteenth-century houses by the towpath, the wisteria hangs its powder blue flowers delicately over the walls, too fastidious to compete with the japonica and burgeoning lilac. Wild duck are flying over the water, the glare from which becomes too intense for the eyes at mid-day. Pleasure launches pass, and the tide is running fast to Richmond. Other birds are active besides the duck – swans deign to accept scraps from the idlers on Magnolia Wharf, while the sparrows (what more enterprising creature than the London sparrow or more diligent in his business?) hop on to floating driftwood – mariners for a moment. Litter of all kinds comes down with the tide – decayed matting, fag packets, branches. A few feet from the towpath floats a lavatory seat and a superannuated contraceptive, the one encircling the other in a last embrace: you, comrades to the end, who have studied the antics of men and women more closely than Krafft-Ebing, tell me your mournful secrets before you are swept out of sight!

In this book, dealing largely with the overlooked joys of London, interest must centre less on the well-known villages and hamlets than on those almost submerged in the later growth of London and generally not considered worth attention.

Clerkenwell is one, together with parts of its larger administrative borough of

Finsbury. There are small areas of Finsbury, especially round St. Luke's, which still possess a hint of village character. St. Luke's is now roofless, but the tower and spire are to remain. Until the recent demolition of St. Luke's Hospital, which had been the Bank of England's Printing Works since the Great War, the view of hospital and church down Old Street had remained practically unaltered since the eighteenth century. Near the church are a few good old shops with slightly curved windows, and the eighteenth-century rectory in Helmet Row has a garden behind. The illusion of being in a country village is almost complete in spring in the view from the churchyard, for the trees cover up inconsistencies and are full of birds, and the churchyard garden is bright with tulips. Recent research has shown that St. Luke's Church was the joint work of Hawksmoor and John James and not of George Dance the Elder. Incidentally, the ironwork round the churchyard is very fine and worth a glance – spears and clusters of spears at the gates and finely designed gas standards, severe and effective, incorporated at intervals in the railings. In the adjoining Caslon Street are terraced houses of early nineteenth-century date, still with shutters. Bartholomew Square is now very decayed; there is a playground in the middle, presided over by the obelisk spire of St. Luke's, like a relic of some ancient civilization. Much of the area was quite rural, even after the building of the hospital in the eighteenth century. At this time, the hospital looked out over open country as far as the hills of Highgate and Hampstead, and at the back of the asylum were bowling greens, a fish pond and a large open-air bathing pond, known as the Peerless Pool, which survived until about 1870 among dwellings that had been erected over the former pleasure grounds. 'The Pleasure Bath of Peerless Pool offering the bather the very advantage he would least expect to find at so short a distance from the centre of the Metropolis' was supplied by springs, probably rising in the region of Hampstead. The old trees disappeared during the various extensions to the hospital made by the Bank.

This pleasure ground was only one of many tea gardens, spas and medicinal springs which, with their accompanying attractions of concert rooms, skittle alleys and grottos, made Clerkenwell popular with Londoners in the eighteenth and early nineteenth centuries. Most of these wells have now been built over, but the springs remain, although covered up, at Sadlers Wells Theatre.

Finsbury was created at the turn of the century by the fusion of several ancient parishes, and Clerkenwell, made up of the parishes of St. James and St. John, is the most important historically. The name comes from Clerks Well, to which the Parish Clerks of London came to perform their yearly miracle play. The well still exists. The church of St. James, with its beautifully proportioned tower and spire, built to the designs of James Carr in 1792, is on the site of the old nunnery occupied by nuns of the Benedictine Order and suppressed by Henry VIII. The fine qualities of the church have been hidden for years by the property surrounding it on Clerkenwell Green. At the time of writing, demolitions round the church have opened up some new and unencumbered views. There is something to be said for the creation of an open space here, but I regret the loss of the little houses and shops. I even regret the hoarding that masked a bombed site; it was crowded with small posters in the late Victorian manner, for though the posters were for car sales, and boxing and wrestling matches, the effect at a distance was just as satisfying as the hoardings of the 1890's. For years, the sudden view of the Green as one turns the corner from the Sessions House has never failed to give me pleasure – the little eighteenth- and early nineteenth-century houses and shops being just sufficient with the mop-like trees to suggest its one-time rural character. Over all, the slender spire of St. James stood on watch, white stone turned to gold in the afternoon sun, and there was, besides, the pleasure of sitting in the little café at a marble-topped table, eating sticky sweet Bakewell tarts, listening to the talk of lorry drivers and gazing across the Green at the men surfacing after a brief visit to the gents.

There is a pretty little pub, the Horseshoe, in Clerkenwell Close – stock brick in the Georgian part, the small Victorian portion being stuccoed, and painted in blue, grey and white. Hemming it in are the grey barrack-like blocks of the Peabody Trust's Clerkenwell Estate. One or two streets of eighteenth-century houses of pleasing character are still to be found in the area round the church; one can only hope they will somehow escape destruction. St. James's Walk, perhaps the best, has been given the benefit of brightly coloured doors in the Chelsea manner. Before leaving the Green, those interested in the grimmer aspects of London history should take a look at the Hugh Myddelton School in Corporation Row. The school, of no architectural distinction in itself, was built on the site of the old House of Detention, the dungeons of which are still to be seen underneath the present building. More interesting still is the school keeper's house, a plain stuccoed building in the angle of the wall, once the residence of the prison governor. The House of Detention, used for prisoners awaiting trial, was the scene of the Fenian outrage in 1867, when Michael Barrett and his associates blew up the prison wall; none of the prisoners escaped, but six people were killed and some one hundred and twenty injured. Barrett was hanged at the Old Bailey in 1868 for the offence, the execution being notable as the last to take place in public in England.

A short walk from Clerkenwell Green (where, incidentally, Henry Carey had the idea for that most charming of old London songs, 'Sally in our Alley', from a 'prentice courtship he encountered here) brings one to Jerusalem Passage. This is a dark, interesting alley, no doubt named after the St. John of Jerusalem public house which stood here in the eighteenth century. Little cafés and 'mixed businesses' line one side of the passage which leads to all that is left of St. John's Square – a few late Georgian houses in a row with a sturdy old shop front at the far end. There is a good view of the old Priory Gate from the end of Jerusalem Passage. The ancient stonework of the gateway and the modern block immediately adjoining make curious neighbours and form as piquant a contrast in architectural styles as could well be imagined. The English offshoot of the Order of St. John of Jerusalem was established in Clerkenwell in the twelfth century, but the monastic buildings belonging to this powerful company have vanished long ago, except for the crypt of the church of St. John. The gatehouse, which has been put to many uses in its time, was built somewhat later, in 1504. The English branch, suppressed in 1540, was revived in 1831, and the gateway restored to the Order in the 1870's.

Goswell Road, where Mr. Pickwick lodged with Mrs. Bardell, is much less salubrious today. This incidentally reminds me of a curious thought I have often had in London of the number of places associated with purely fictional characters, a consideration applying especially to Dickens's creations. On occasions, often for commercial ends, these associations are themselves based on guesswork only, and therefore become fictional in a double sense . . . the London that never was. Off Goswell Road are the derelict terraces of Powell Street, now in process of demolition and rebuilding, and the woebegone houses at one end of Sebastian Street, where rotting shutters move in the wind eerily and political announcements are fly-posted on the jambs of empty doors and sightless windows: 'Mosley Speaks. Islington Green. Sunday' – the same mothy old pre-war ingredients all over again. Northampton Square is worth inspection, and much like the Bloomsbury squares in character, even to the solicitors who occupy some of the best houses. The great circular garden – one of the best kept in industrialized London – has lawns and flowerbeds under tall trees and urns full of lobelia and geraniums. But the companionable old houses are overpowered by blocks of flats, and the square (circus would be a more accurate term) has lost its architectural unity and somehow its heart. George Baxter, who perfected a process of colour printing from engraved blocks, lived here in a house which, when I last saw it, had become utterly mournful and decayed.

It is extraordinary how many Londons there are. I refer not to those which lie in layers each on top of another, like the various Troys, but to those areas which have gradually become the centre of an interest or trade – cabinet making in Bethnal Green, for instance, jewellery, clock and instrument making in Clerkenwell, greeting cards in certain streets off the Liverpool Road and the rag trades east of Aldgate and in Marylebone. Such areas can be multiplied almost indefinitely. Again there are those districts within districts, with well defined limits – those of the Inns of Court, for example. These various Londons abutting on and cutting across one another make food for speculation, as does the way in which London must appear to those operating its enterprises. To the big caterers, I imagine the city must be seen as a limitless succession of superloaves, country fresh pies and gliding trays – London seen through a Swiss roll. And I wonder how London appears to the light ladies of Soho, Lisle Street and Swedenborg Square: I imagine the tarts view the town as a mere framework, run up by humane persons to provide facilities for the exercise of their ancient profession.

Typical of the sudden transitions of London is the contrast between Hamilton Terrace with its select stucco villas, especially fine on an April evening when the prunus and magnolias are out, and Hamilton Gardens, both in St. John's Wood. Hamilton Gardens is a street of red brick, milk bottles, Gothic doors and tiled paths, like the back streets of a Northern seaside resort; it is, in fact, pure Blackpool – only the cards with the legend 'Apartments' are missing. A single turn unexpectedly brings you into a little backwater of a pleasurable, old-fashioned kind – Alma Square, possessing a post office that might be in any country village and a pretty pub of the same order, the Heroes of Alma. Next comes Nugent Terrace, also with a country town air about it, where you will find a pre-Great War dairy, altogether agreeable, with a tiled landscape below the window – The Devonshire Dairy.

I have mentioned Strand-on-the-Green as a favourite hamlet on the more salubrious parts of the river. Next, for strong contrast, in the industrialized reaches, some mention might be made of Rotherhithe, a district that, after having laid hold of the affections, never lets go, making the victim peevish and irritable if obliged to live elsewhere. Residence by the river in Rotherhithe is a unique experience, completely disabling one for other ways of life. Readers of my book *The London Nobody Knows* may recollect the brief mention of my, now famous, old house there, 'The Little Midshipman', 59, Rotherhithe Street, which may have gone by the time this book appears. That wonderful old house with its sloping floors, odd rooms, pine-panelled kitchen, the bow window with its magnificent views over the river, those sunsets smouldering in dusty scarlet over Wapping, and the swans, carrying their cygnets pic-a-back, who paddled under the bathroom window at high tide for their daily supply of sliced superloaf!

Even when, regrettably, those old houses have gone, much will remain to make an exploration worthwhile. The part round the church still conveys a hint of village character, as well it might, for this small area, the heart of the old hamlet of Redriff, has been remarkably resistant to change, sandwiched in between the great warehouses and wharves on the river side and Bermondsey flats on the other. Blackbirds warble in the churchyard, competing with river noises, and sparrows twitter in the lime trees, the deep green depths of which are humming with bees; in the sun the vivid green forms a pleasing harmony with grey brickwork. There were tulips in the churchyard on my last visit on a hot afternoon in May, and the scent of wallflowers drifted agreeably across the grass. Brightly painted swings and slides in the playground beside the tower add a touch of youthful gaiety to the sober old church and its surrounding buildings, a liveliness that is heightened momentarily by a small boy going down a slide with his transistor set playing. Inside the church, all is still apart from the ticking of the clock in the tower and the vocal efforts of the choir of sparrows in the eaves. Four great columns support the ceiling, each containing (under the plaster) the trunk of an oak tree.

It was from Rotherhithe that the *Mayflower* sailed for Plymouth to embark the Pilgrim Fathers: her owners and crew were mainly local men, and she was ultimately broken up in the Rotherhithe yards. Three of the syndicate of four men owning the *Mayflower*, Robert Childe, John Moore and Christopher Jones, the ship's master, were associated with the church. Yet another famous ship found her end in Rotherhithe – 'The Fighting Temeraire', the subject of Turner's memorable painting in which the veteran of Trafalgar is being towed by paddle tugs to her last berth in Beatson's Yard at Globe Stairs. Some of the oak from her timbers was used to make the altar and altar rails of St. Paul's Church. The close associations between the *Mayflower* and the parish church would seem to make St. Mary's an essential item in the itinerary of a visitor from the States: failure to include it amounts almost to an un-American activity. Other considerations, apart from the sober beauty of the eighteenth-century church (the tower and spire, also eighteenth-century, came later – Londoners were notably reluctant to part with their medieval towers), give special interest to St. Mary's – the romantic story of the gentle Pacific Islander, Prince Lee Boo, and that of the great engineer, Sir Marc Brunel, who came to worship here with his family during the construction of his tunnel under the Thames.

Opposite the church is the Victorian rectory, where, in my Rotherhithe days, one was ushered into a cosy study, lined with books and bric-a-brac, as a rector's sanctum ought to be: there were college photographs of the 'nineties in Oxford frames and a feeling of scholarly security: the atmosphere was compounded of Victorian Oxford and Barchester. Immediately adjoining the rectory is the pretty little eighteenth-century school house with its two charming figures of a boy and girl on brackets corbelled out from the wall. The school, founded under the will of Peter Hills, a well-to-do mariner, still flourishes elsewhere in the parish, and the eighteenth-century school house is now used for social work.

In this riverside backwater, the view of the church, rectory and school against a background of trees, flour mills and the tall warehouses bordering the river and its dark, damp alleyways has a character very much its own, imbued with a flavour of the old nautical ballads of 'Tom Bowling' and 'The Jolly Waterman'.

Even today, Dibdin would be perfectly at home in this part of Bermondsey. At the time of writing, the old house actually named 'The Jolly Waterman' still survives near my own in Rotherhithe Street. 'The Jolly Waterman' was a pub years ago, and after the publication of my previous book, I had a most interesting letter from a reader who often visited the place in the early 1920's, describing the cosy shrimp teas on winter evenings there, the joy of tightly drawn curtains muffling the river sounds that floated up in the darkness, firelight and the mingled smells of tar, flour and spices. Also near the church are the parish Engine and Watch Houses, dating from the early 1820's. Body snatching was rife at this period and not in the dark riverside churchyards only. The resurrection men operated even in central London. The church of St. Sepulchre without Newgate had its Watch House up to its destruction during the war (a replica forming the modern rectory has replaced it); the corpses were auctioned off to the highest bidders at the Fortune of War public house in Cock Lane.

From the old hamlet of Redriff, a short walk of a few hundred yards brings us back into present day Bermondsey – all dust, fruit, record players and pregnant, pram-pushing women. A small deposit secures any article and the kids are Lone Rangers. Snack bars and eating places are here – Bill's, Jax and those with more fancy names, such as 'The Albion'. Scrubbed tables, worn linoleum, gaslight and scraps of lace curtain are essential fittings to such dining-rooms; other equipment includes faded photographs, greyhound racing posters and statuettes of the Queen. Gigantic sauce bottles loom large over the thick cups, the rough bottoms of which persuade one into the belief that unusual amounts of sugar remain there undissolved. Faded woodwork, blistered by the sun in 1910, a variety of homely chairs and huge ashtrays are more or less standard in these interiors. Menus are chalked up, offering such delicacies as:—

> Roast Beef 2 Veg. 2/1d. (Yorkshire 2d.)
> Baked Jam Roll. Plain & Syrup. Plain & Jam.
> Rice & Custard. Rice & Jam. Plain & Marmalade.

Wimbledon is my favourite starting point for Putney and Fulham – the old village of Wimbledon adjoining the common, parts of which have a character reminiscent of Hampstead. The old pharmacy has now gone and its early nineteenth-century Jacobean building is turned into a club, but there are several pretty boxes of houses near the church, the charming Express Dairy illustrated on page 67, an Edwardian confectioner's shop and a veterinary surgeon's Victorian Gothic house, complete with projecting lamp and a pair of lions guarding the door. Old Wimbledon can be expected to improve as time goes on, a local society having been formed to tidy the village up. The Wimbledon at the foot of the hill is of modern growth, or at least since the 1880's, though by no means devoid of interest, especially in the matter of pubs and the Wimbledon Theatre, which is Edwardian Baroque at the end of its life. The theatre's entrance hall is full of marble, mahogany and brass, and there is a great fireplace (the Edwardian age was comfortably inclined) still with its leather-padded fender.

The road to Putney flanks the side of the common. Not much of a village character is left in Putney. The Victorians built the district up, as they did in Fulham, with endless streets of terraced houses, most of them apparently out of the same mould, and recent developments are completing the process. Even the Victorian architecture is going, for on Putney Hill the great villas, inseparably connected in the mind with pale governesses, billiard rooms, skivvies heaving buckets of coal and obsequious tradesmen, are being sold to provide building sites. Characterless flats are taking their place, and 'The Pines', surely the last stronghold of correct Victorian behaviour, has had a new block of flats clapped next to it. But the wooden seat in St. John's Avenue remains with its inscription 'For Wounded Soldiers', a relic of the Great War. These changes, inevitable under present conditions, make the work of imagining the figures of Swinburne and Watts-Dunton and their domestic life much more difficult; Swinburne, the masochist, dragooned into conformity at last, too late to become Poet Laureate, occasionally eluding his guard and staggering back drunk from Wimbledon village. I have always believed that the ultimate refuge for the revolutionary is to conform. It may be that all revolutions harbour a perverse desire to bring this about – but the centrally-heated contemporary blocks of a well-shod society – that is too bad!

> If you were Queen of pleasure,
> And I were King of pain
> We'd hunt down love together,
> Pluck out his flying feather
> And find his mouth a rein;
> If you were Queen of pleasure
> And I were King of pain.

Only the most determined collector of metropolitan delights would venture into Fulham. There is, at least superficially, a soul-chilling cheerlessness in those monotonous streets of drab houses in the area round North End Road and Munster Road, where a coloured population has infiltrated and where the motor-bikes, shrouded like phantoms, lurk behind privets in mouldy gardens. As late as the middle of the last century, Fulham was a place of market gardens, and other-wise consisted of four villages – the old Fulham round the parish church, Parson's Green, North End and Walham Green, with a number of private residences dotted about. One of these was 'The Grange', home of Burne-Jones. In the

biography of her husband, Lady Burne-Jones gives a depressing picture of the gradual encroachment of the deadly streets. Most of this building took place between 1850 and the turn of the twentieth century. For my part, I am not greatly affected by drabness, provided it be London drabness, and in consequence rather enjoy the monotonous villas, each with its bay window and bit of debased carving. I like the tiled paths, the television sets topped with vases of plastic flowers, the street market at North End and, most of all, after a home match, to watch the steady stream of sad-faced men returning from an afternoon's football through the streets surrounding the Bishop's Park: the English take their pleasures badly.

Fulham has a few late Victorian pubs still more or less intact – one of the best being opposite the church. The entrance to the huge saloon bar is under an arch of glazed terra-cotta encrusted with music-hall baroque decorations. Inside (and these are a feature common to other Fulham pubs) are semi-circular snuggeries, big and lined with leather. Practically all the fittings of this bar are original, apart from the electric light shades, which, as usual, strike a false note. Traces of rural Fulham can be found along the New King's Road, where the early Industrial Revolution architecture of the Fulham Pottery makes a picturesque group, made to measure for artists. A yard, slightly grass-grown in places, cobbled in others, leads to an interesting range of buildings with kilns breaking the roof line like huge ginger beer bottles. (North Kensington was also once famous for its potteries, the site being commemorated by Pottery Lane, near Walmer Lane, Notting Hill, where a kiln is still to be seen behind a high wall.) The Fulham Pottery was founded in 1671 by John Dwight, master potter. Piles of stoneware bottles of traditional character are examples of the continuing craftsmanship of the pottery; a few Victorian charcoal filters in the Gothic style are dotted about with pictorial effect. Not far from here are remnants of the old village architecture of Fulham, a double-fronted house of late Georgian date and a Regency cottage covered with wisteria, both oddly at variance with their present-day surroundings. Some evidence of the one-time rural aspect of the neighbourhood is obtained from the row of eighteenth-century terraced houses a little farther along with the date plaque 1738, named Elysium Row: no doubt this was a more truthful description in the mid-eighteenth century, when fields stretched away in front of the terrace to the river and its picturesque bridge.

A few old houses of good appearance remain on Parson's Green, left high and dry when the surrounding gardens were submerged by the nineteenth-century developers. For those interested in following up the scattered remains of de-molished City churches – a rewarding and unusual approach to London per-ambulating – the church of St. Dionis on Parson's Green preserves the font and pulpit from the church of St. Dionis Backchurch, a Wren building which disappeared from the Lime Street area in the nineteenth century. St. Dionis, Parson's Green, was built by Ewan Christian in 1886. It is of brick and stone in a commonplace Gothic, but its Wren fittings give the place a special interest.

Hoxton, already mentioned in connection with its music hall past, has, in spite of the huge blocks of flats everlastingly mushrooming from the little streets, considerable traces of the old East End village life. The music hall apart, Hoxton Street, lined with market stalls, is a place of pilgrimage for those in search of the genuine East End, especially on Saturday afternoon. It is all cabbages and pregnant women, cabbages and pregnant women again, Sammy Davis Jnr. at the Coconut Grove, 'Sorry to hear about Flo', 'Take yer bloody mawleys off them comics', cut-price shampoo, cut-price cornflakes, cut-price everything. On the pet stalls are budgies rocking themselves to sleep in spite of the din in the upper stories of their chromium residences. A mongrel puppy pleads with melting eyes from a straw-lined box. He is offering devotion with all his might, but nobody wants it today. Nevertheless, the anxious heart continues to hope, though by the end of the afternoon the eyes have become sad. Top ten tunes scream from the record stalls. Toy stalls abound, and you can buy shoes so villainously pointed that only the Devil could get a foot into them. Jellied eels, loved by Hoxton people, can be eaten in a tiled and mirrored establishment with marble-topped tables. Fish and chips are also a delicacy much esteemed in Hoxton Street, often rounded off by an iced lolly. And when the jostling and pushing, buying and selling comes to an end, when the music stops, there is the undertaker's at your service. There is a perspex cross in the window and the announcement 'Sanitary Preservation of the Dead' in black and gold lettering. This proves how well Hoxton Street caters for all contingencies. 'Sanitary Preservation of the Dead' has a business-like finality about it that does no good to the morbid streak in my nature; it is less appealing than the betting shops, the butchers' stalls, less perhaps than the Coconut Grove. Pregnant women and undertakers have this much in common: they form the entrances and exits to Hoxton, and the system has spread everywhere else.

Hoxton Street is worth a special visit, if only to see the rich Edwardian lamps (the base of one is in the drawing on page 71). These are early examples destined to disappear. At the tops, the trumpet-shaped shades supported between two brackets suggest tall, headless women foolishly trying on hats. A tour of Hoxton will reveal much in the way of desiccated old houses and odd collectors' items – at least for the present; in time most of old Hoxton will disappear. Charles Square, a turning or two off Old Street, is one of these dilapidated parts of Hoxton. The garden is nothing but a bald patch, where a little hopeless grass struggles for existence in a half-hearted way, and some disillusioned privets. Some fine plane trees remain, rustling mournfully out of respect for the death of the square. Flats and offices fill all the sides, except for the eighteenth-century house occupied by the National Union of Tailors and Garment Workers. The house has a well-tailored door with a shapely fanlight, in which the glazing bars are arranged to accommodate a central lamp, now disappeared. Hoxton Square is ruinous and industrialized, though the garden in the centre is pleasant in the shade of a great plane tree and there are standard roses. One or two roughly used houses in a broken down condition remain.

Hoxton is a good point of departure for Stoke Newington, Edmonton and those other villages a day's coachride from town in the time of Charles Lamb, but now almost as much a part of London as Islington. Stoke Newington was once considered a stage in the rise to wealth of the Jewish community, and may still be, the pattern being a progression from Aldgate to Stoke Newington, Golders Green or Maida Vale, finally to Hampstead or St. John's Wood. Today Stoke Newington has become a home for coloured immigrants, though Woolworths still display a variety of cards for the Jewish New Year. Moving up to Stoke Newington, one passes the terraces of the New North Road. These are badly decayed at the Hoxton end, though once inhabited by people of some position. Now they are quite deplorable. The canal forms a boundary, the houses at the Islington end having come up in the world after a period of decline. Next come the porticoed terraces of Southgate Road and endless brick boxes of villas in the grids of the surrounding streets, acres of them, all more or less identical – the classic ruins of Hackney, where, as in Fulham and East Dulwich, draped motor-bikes serve as ornaments in the front gardens. Then into Kingsland Road and Kingsland High Street, a lively area – especially the street market in Ridley Road at weekend. Savour on Saturday the cooked eel shops, the establishments where they sell flash clothes, those richly Victorian pubs. Dark skins and bleached blondes weave in and out of the slow moving crowd, dreadful ties catch the eye and garments that could only be worn by English women stun the imagination: it is an earthly paradise of chewing gum, oranges and pop records.

Clissold Park, the river and above all its ancient church combine with the remaining old houses to give a definite village character to Stoke Newington; a suggestion of being in a country town that neither the building developments of the late Victorian age nor recent rebuilding entirely disrupt. Early in the nineteenth century, the village comprised little more than the houses round the church, those along Church Street, parts of the High Street and a few on the Green. The Manor of Stoke Newington is recorded in Domesday Book as being the property of the Canons of St. Paul's Cathedral, in whose possession it still remains. There are three fine houses of the early eighteenth century in High Street that give us an idea of how attractive the place must have been when Defoe lived in the village. One stands close to the street and the others are set back. Two

Hoxton Saturday afternoon

are in use. The remaining house has locked gates, tall pillars with stucco peeling and decaying, and urns. The ground floor windows are boarded up, so is the door, a carved door of some quality. Its garden was full of willow herb and cone flowers last time I passed. I thought the old, dark house might be full of secrets: one might hear the swish of dresses long since fallen into dust or meet the phantom of a coquette upon the stairs.

Until one reaches the unfortunate town hall, Church Street is very pleasing. The new church is by Scott and when built must have appeared to the villagers as an outpost of Victorian suburban progress. It is in strange contrast to the old church opposite, to the proportions and character of which no attention was evidently paid. Still the spire, completed much later, has more vitality than many by Scott. The ancient St. Mary's is a delightful place and is on a site occupied by a church since Anglo-Saxon times. The South aisle was built in 1563 by the Lord of the Manor. Barry enlarged the church in 1829, and the timber spire also dates from this period. Old St. Mary's was damaged in 1940 and restored in 1953. Stoke Newington Church Street has late eighteenth-century terraces with good carved doors; some of the houses in the street would be more attractive if they had escaped being turned to commercial purposes. A village-type post office is to be found here, comparable to that in Alma Square already mentioned and the pocket-sized one in Lisson Grove. The Stoke Newington post office is also a newsagent's, and I was delighted to see current copies of *Smart Novels* and *Christian Novels* on sale. My mother favoured these charming publications (what could be more period nowadays than the word 'smart'?) when I was a small boy, and I, always ready to read everything within sight, devoured them myself. I can remember, even at that age, pondering on the subtle implications of 'smart' as opposed to 'christian'. . . . Such periodicals are a joy to see in these present times. My hope is that they will go on for ever, gradually becoming more and more out of step with the horrible future.

Here, too, are little sweetshops where one can buy those time-honoured delights – liquorice, chocolate bananas and sherbet fountains. There are also those gift bags which I, with an inflamed imagination, found a trifle disappoint-ing. But today's lucky bags, bulky and king-sized, with names like 'The Out of this World Gift Bag' or 'The Wild West Surprise Bag', address themselves to a harder-to-please generation, and know better than to fall down on the job. In these windows, I was pleased to renew my acquaintance with the jelly babies, dolly mixtures, the pale-looking chocolate buttons and toffee cigarettes.

But the sugar pigs and sugar whistles were not: I fear they belong only to yesterday.

FIVE

London Peculiar:
the Joys of the Streets

———————— * ————————

THE JOYS of the London streets – the free entertainments – though neither so widespread nor so varied nowadays as at former periods, are nonetheless still sufficiently rich to delight the London fancier. They fall into two main categories: human and architectural. The greatest loss is in those who get a living off the London streets: no doubt there was a great deal of misery behind those sellers of fresh milk, watercress, hot pies or gingerbread: a life-consuming struggle on the part of the match boys, the vendors of penny toys and the violet sellers, whose melancholy can be felt in the old photographs. All the same, London thoroughfares are the poorer for their passing. I have a collection of toys bought, some for my mother, others later for myself, off the Holborn pavements in front of the Prudential – a climbing monkey with fez, a toy chocolate machine and a choral top, the tune of which changes as the top spins . . . what charming days those were for lucky children in London. But the magic is not quite faded, for though the toy men have vanished from Holborn and Ludgate Hill, you can still find them in the foyers of the Regent Street shops in the weeks before Christmas on Saturday evenings. And the clockwork toys are put through their paces on the ground, just as they used to be. In a way I am glad those pathetic hawkers have gone, for they depressed my childhood fearfully. I remember when very little buying a doll for fourpence from a poor old soul, blue with cold: I decided to love it, and carried it home on top of a tram, but to no purpose: the doll, you see, had been carved from a block of Castile soap, and might not have a clean bill of health. I sobbed my heart out when it went behind the fire, thinking of the forlorn old figure on the rainy corner. . . . I am rather glad those pathetic creatures have gone.

I love religious cranks. One day it is my plan to form a collection of cranky tracts given away in the streets of London. There will be nothing in them (of course) about the real work done all over London by those not ashamed to confess the crucified and risen Christ, but there will be lots of crummy fun. I miss the fat old woman and the two men who used to haul a harmonium out of a small van on

Tower Hill, sing 'The Church's One Foundation' and proceed to tell their audience about the Second Coming. They are always so sure of themselves and so satisfied, these fanatics: in fact, the prospect of the Second Coming seems not to frighten them. My own view is that this event must be indefinitely postponed, for in those appalling circumstances even the pamphleteers will be too busy to assist the rest of us.

Many of the finest religious cranks of London find their way to Epsom for the Derby Day: there you may study them in optimum conditions, and hear their rallying cry, 'Don't put your money on a horse – put it on the Lord Jesus Christ Who is always a winner!'

When Ella Shields died, it was said that her character of Burlington Bertie had been preserved only in her music hall song – that he disappeared long ago, the last of the shabby genteel men. This is not so, for one day not long ago I watched from a car the most perfect specimen of the genus in Oxford Street. He was garbed in a shiny old suit of 1920 vintage that had once come from the cellars of Sackville Street. A ten-day beard covered his greasy chin, and his toes, blacked out with boot polish, peered from indescribable boots. He carried an old brolly, the ferrule of which was sharpened to a point which he used with enviable ease to transfer fag ends into his left hand and thence to his pocket. Broken up and reconstituted, these dockers are made into packets of tramps' cigarettes, a choice item of commerce among London hobos and about the only kind of cigarette I have not yet sampled.

Another favourite character of mine is the tipster in Tavistock Square. Rain or shine, I have seen him there for the last twenty years, always on the same pitch by the railings, and he has a selection of racehorse drawings on display – his own, I imagine. He certainly adds interest to this rather dull corner of Southampton Row, a thoroughfare that I class among the less inspiring in central London, the Hotels Russell and Imperial always excepted.

Those readers of *The London Nobody Knows* will remember the pleasure I have in Queenie of St. John's Wood and her owner with the gramophone. Dogs are essential in the street hawkers' business, especially among the English whose love of the canine tribes is the secret of their supremacy among Europeans. On the opposite page I have drawn another dog and gramophone outfit occasionally to be seen in the West End in the neighbourhood of Bond Street, Piccadilly and Trafalgar Square. The gramophone was once considered too easy a way of earning a musical livelihood off the streets. To the older generations that remembered the German Bands, the harpists and those who drew music most mournful from the one-string or Chinese fiddle, the gramophone seemed beneath contempt. Nowadays it is quite acceptable, especially if an old horn model be rigged up on a bassinet and the whole thing a picturesque, perambulating ruin – but I wonder why

no enterprising street musician has (on the same easy principle) thought of merely playing a transistor set perched on a pram in traditional fashion? One of my favourite characters is the lady seen occasionally in the Strand, wearing a knitted hat, smoking a cigarette and nonchalantly playing a violin from behind a music stand. Street singing is seldom worthy of the name nowadays, having degenerated, often enough, into a mere cover for begging, but occasionally at Waterloo Station the rush hour is made melodious by the playing of a flute, quite expertly if a little sharp, by a small man with a melancholy face and an overcoat down to his ankles.

It was in South London that I drew the poor old fellow opposite, a figure in a derelict street, full of uneasiness somehow, like the Ancient Mariner. Most of the great London termini are good for those whose pleasure it is to search out the misfits of London, the best time being late on a Saturday evening. Tramps of the sort I have illustrated lie down in dark corners, no doubt hoping to be run in by the police (so getting a night's free lodging), and strange figures, unknown to working day London, come out on their mysterious errands. One station is haunted by a figure known as 'The Woman in White' – a silent being dressed in white from head to foot who carries an open white umbrella. Poor, pathetic, old, women rag-pickers fish for scraps of food in garbage cans round the stations and the great markets. A few months ago, I watched an appalling old woman suffering from syphilis being forcibly kissed by two tramps on a dark, little used staircase in central London. First they snatched away the sandwich she was desolately chewing, then they kissed her against her will. As nothing worse ensued, I decided not to intervene, giving her half-a-crown and thinking that neither in life nor in Hogarth or Petronius had I encountered a scene so degraded.

In my previous book, I mentioned the street photographers – not the smart operators with modern equipment, but the old-fashioned kind I had entirely given up for lost. I imagined they had gone out with the carte-de-visite, but I was wrong. I found such a photographer when crossing Westminster Bridge on my way to my seat in the Abbey for Princess Alexandra's wedding. The better to interview him, I commissioned a couple of photographs – two and six each or two for four shillings. I had the two for four shillings 'and for pity's sake, don't make me too much like Dracula'. I told my man I had not seen many of his kind about. 'No, you won't find another like me in London, sir – they've all gone. That's why I'm the last one and I'm seventy. Twenty-five quid a year I pay for my licence to the Westminster Council and my pitch is from here to Boadicea. Used to work the fairs and races, but I don't now. Move up a bit this way, if you please, sir, then I can get you in front of Big Ben. They all like to be in front of Big Ben.' So he adjusted his equipment – camera, bulb, tripod and little tin of hypo. Within a minute my photographs were complete – direct positives – the image appearing as he rubbed the prints with a mysterious liquid on his finger.

Old man singing in
a derelict street

'No, these photographs won't fade, sir – you're thinking of the old tin-types we used to get sent across from 'Merica. Just wash it when you get home . . . don't be afraid, just wash it . . . don't be frightened . . . it's the bromide that does it, the bromide.' The resulting small photographs were wonderfully yellow and brown – already like a faded chlorobromide of the 1860's and low in tone, too – something foggy – myself and Big Ben in a London particular. One can be found reproduced among the printed ephemera of London on the dust wrapper of this book. Admittedly the day was misty, but hardly so soup-like it seemed to me . . . after all it *was* an April morning. Years ago, I remember, these photographs were supplied in a paper frame. On this occasion, they were handed to me enfolded in sheets of thin paste board. All through the Abbey service I was haunted by the fear that the photographs (awaiting washing) were fading in my pocket. I therefore took an early opportunity to inspect and wash them in the Abbey's lavatory. To my relief, they were still intact. But he had certainly made me look like Dracula.

One of my greatest joys in the City is the queer little building on the opposite page, once a Turkish bath and to be found near St. Botolph's Churchyard. In spring the churchyard is one of the most agreeable spots in the City, when the pigeons are out on the lawns at tea time or squinting from the urns by the church door, when the flower beds are tulip bright and the magnolia is out. Industrious sparrows hop and sway on the branches of the trees lining the path – feathery smudges of sooty brown moving in and out of the green haze of opening leaves. City lovers, loosed from offices, walk arm in arm under the gas brackets spanning the path, and those not in a hurry for the evening trains sit on benches, reading or watching the tennis players. There is St. Botolph's church hall, a delightful Palladian building with statues of charity children – boy and girl – in niches. After this is the King's Arms and then the unexpected, pretty tiled building once the entrance to Neville's Turkish Baths, the faded plate of which remains on the door. Inside, at the top of the staircase leading to the baths below, are panels of stained glass in peacock blue and gold. This Moorish building is of pale duck-egg blue and darker blue (sobered down a little by the London dirt) in tiles striped and banded and also in brown, cream and gold coloured tiles. The onion-shaped dome is topped by a crescent and star. The door of terracotta is a rich example of this kind of work, and would not be out of place in the Alhambra: it has deeply cut capitals supporting a Moorish arch. Below ground, the baths are still intact and very eloquent of vanished City days when a corpulent company director would while away an afternoon and a little avoirdupois in those exotic surroundings, before taking himself to his green and pleasant villa on Denmark Hill. Today the baths are used by a bank for storage purposes.

After the baths comes the Natural Form Boot Company – 'Bespoke Boot Maker' in gold below the window – delightfully period, and farther down still is

Turkish Baths, Bishopsgate

Millingen's, the umbrella shop, full of gold lettering on glass inside, richly Victorian and a gem for the collector. The shop has two poles, each decorated with the head of Punchinello, outside the door; even the window blinds are period; they are lettered all over and carry the announcement 'Umbrella and Parasol Manufacturer'.

Also of terracotta is the building illustrated opposite and on page 83, which houses the branch of the Westminster Bank in Chancery Lane. It was once the ill-fated Birkbeck Bank. As rebuilding is foreshadowed, it must eventually disappear – that is if it has not already done so by the time this book is in print. However, this extraordinary building is worth recording in any event. The fantasy apparent in the drawing is heightened in reality by the material used – glazed faience in yellow and bright pale blue. It is impossible to say what style of architecture has been employed. The architect gave his clients full value for money, and its cost must have been enormous even in the nineteenth century. This bride's cake erection comprises all the variants of the Classical styles. There are arabesques, fluted column piled on column, caryatides, sunken panels, elaborate cornices and, for good measure, portraits in relief of celebrated Victorians. This portrait gallery includes Tennyson, Bessemer, Brunel and Edison. Finally, there are great groups of symbolic statuary – muscular females in flowing draperies and helmets representing Britannia and other personifications, handing out largesse to crouching and (presumably) less fortunate peoples. All of which is highly entertaining, and in fact the whole building can be read off as a sort of pictorial Samuel Smiles – an encouragement to succeed in the teeth of appalling difficulties. Needless to say, in the best Victorian tradition, the structure is thoroughly well built, every inch of it. Dr. Birkbeck, himself, figures among the portraits, and the name of the bank appears in faded characters in the tower above the entrance. The domed banking hall is – or was – particularly splendid. No doubt the building will be replaced by yet another office block of which London has already had more than enough. One understands that such architectural fantasies are hard to clean under present conditions and also chronically wasteful of space; nonetheless the steady elimination of these entertaining examples of Victoriana is rubbing out all that gave variety and character to the London streets.

While on the subject of banks, there is a small but rather attractive building in Mayfair (until recently partly occupied by Barclays Bank and now the premises of a famous firm of antique dealers) worth mentioning here, No. 39 Brook Street. At a time when so much of the West End is in danger of being demolished and after so much has changed beyond recognition, it is good to know that one of its remaining Regency buildings has been the subject of careful preservation. This is a house possessing not only architectural quality, but also historic interest. It is, moreover, one of the few genuinely haunted houses in London. Some time

MINSTER BANK

Westminster Bank Chancery Lane Branch

about 1820 it was the residence of Sir Jeffrey Wyattville, a contemporary of Nash and perhaps best known for the substantial amount of remodelling he carried out at Windsor Castle. Not far away, at what is now No. 25, was the residence of Handel. Most of the ghostly visitations have taken place on the upper floors. Sounds of fighting and brawling have been heard on the top of a staircase and the sound of a body falling down it, although nothing was to be seen. Shadowy figures have been felt passing along corridors, and on the ground floor, in the rooms occupied by the bank, a spectral hand was felt on a shoulder. An old woman, dressed in black and seated on a chair, faded quickly out of sight, to the horror of a girl employed in the building who mistook the phantom for a customer. All this, of course, raises the query as to what the apparitions hope to achieve by their unwelcome visits. . . .

There are two other free entertainments in Mayfair that can be added in this chapter – one, on Sundays only, is the open air exhibition on the railings of the Green Park from the station to a point roughly opposite the Cavalry Club, and the other is the electricity station in Brown Hart Gardens. Both are within a few minutes' walk of Brook Street.

The Green Park academy makes no pretension to rivalling its near neighbour, the Royal Academy. It resembles in some ways the annual open-air exhibition in the Embankment Gardens and certainly adds spice to a Sunday morning stroll in Piccadilly. Bearded, duffle-coated artists stand talking by the pavement edge, a wary eye on potential customers. Some sport shooting brakes, carrying their wares in them after the manner of regular street market traders. Many of the pictures thus exhibited are indifferent enough – either feebly abstract or crummily cottage: over most hangs an indefinable suggestion of art shops – those establishments that have gone all abstract, though retaining their old loyalty to decorated mirrors, ghastly reading lamps, biscuit barrels and poker work. The whole ensemble is a sort of poor relation of the Bond Street dealers a stone's throw away. Spontaneous, unorganized shows like this seem less natural here than in Paris: there is some settled principle in the nature of London which makes this kind of affair out of character, like a Bishop in an underwear shop. But it is all good fun: some of the paintings are worth looking at and a few find purchasers.

My own inclination, however, is for the genuine pavement art – the lighthouses, waterfalls and portraits of the Saviour. Transcriptions of Walt Disney and of American cartoon characters generally are right out. I must have kippers and the Virgin Mary. Had I rooms large enough to take them, I should commission some specially on material more portable than paving stones. Were I a millionaire, my time would not be spent in collecting Impressionist paintings at ludicrous prices; I should form a collection of old enamel advertisements, buying from off their original walls all those found in good condition – those for Hudson's Soap, Matchless Polish, Nestlé's Milk, Van Houten's or Epp's Cocoa. I should have them framed in the manner of oil paintings, and command that they be hung round the walls of my board rooms. And if fellow directors failed to admire them, I should immediately reconstitute the Board. Not to do so would be to run the risk of not being talked about in the Clubs, which is even worse than being talked about.

The electricity station in Brown Hart Gardens is purest Edwardian Baroque. There are two domed pavilions, one each end, heavy with cornices, swags and Roman Ionic columns. 'Free Classic' is what the Edwardians called it as they dumped it all over London: Norman Shaw had a hand in the creation of the style, followed by others whose experience of the classic styles was, at best, perfunctory. In time, people may come to praise it; it is certainly coarse and vulgar enough to find admirers. Between the two pavilions, on top of the raised terrace which links them together, is the Duke Street Garden, a cold, dreary,

Boy on Sea horse
Birkbeck Bank

paved area, chiefly visited by pigeons. I always look upon it as the dullest garden in London. Notices in Edwardian frames prohibit a variety of activities under the bye-laws – fighting, brawling, quarrelling, shouting, playing with cards or dice, singing and the practice of gymnastics. I cannot imagine anyone, even the daring young man on the flying trapeze celebrated in the Victorian song, indulging in gymnastics in so unlikely a spot, not even in the Mayfair of Mr. Michael Arlen. . . . No idle or disorderly person or person in an intoxicated, unclean or verminous condition is allowed in the garden, so it is well to give oneself a quick appraisement before setting out.

I am often asked what I consider to be the ugliest or most monstrous building in London. My answer, after long experience and certain changes of mind, is now always the same: Windsor House in Victoria Street. In the midst of alterations in this deadliest of thoroughfares, there is at least one building which I hope will remain intact, and it is this Windsor House, the ugliest customer, I believe, in London – Gargantuan, Brobdingnagian, utterly impossible. A drawing of it will be found opposite. It is a safe thing to prophesy that its like will never appear again in London. I love bad architecture if it be gloriously, splendidly, actively bad (none of your emasculated, thin-blooded badness) in the same way that I like bad paintings. Windsor House has delighted me for years, and I often go out of my way just to enjoy it. Drawing it gave me unusual satisfaction. Everything that could be done to debauch classic details has been done – with knobs on. That pair of elephantine columns apparently in the process of being squashed by the sheer weight of the superincumbent masonry, that clumsy ornament, those unfeeling, gross proportions! As I drew, a long frieze of maidens passed by – no Panathenic procession, they, but tourists, scantily clad, youth escorted. The big bosoms of the girls seemed to constantly float across my eyes like a balloon race and to harmonize with the architecture.

There is something of the pre-war super-cinema about Windsor House. In fact, the whole façade resembles a set from some gigantic Biblical epic, some sure-fire box office draw, an all-star super special picture of the year. One of the most charming Victorian pubs adjoins Windsor House, the Albert at the corner of Palmer Street: rich glass below and pretty, white-painted iron balconies above. This contrast between the worst and best Victorian architecture is very striking. Almost opposite is my pet block of Victorian flats – Artillery Mansions – in the Gothic manner. Peer in under the high pointed arch and admire the lonely, gloomy fountain playing in the shadowed courtyard, and think of all those retired military men who must have gone through that portal to their clubs in the sunset days of Empire, boring each other to death with uninteresting recollections from the depths of leather armchairs.

Mention of cinemas and officers brings me to another example of London

WINDSOR
HOUSE

58 Sketch
Victoria Street

peculiar – the Globe Cinema, Putney, illustrated opposite. It is, of all things, Indian, in blue and silver. The domes are like the solar topees of the British Raj. The whole is a feast of off-beat London. As I made my drawing, I noticed several Eastern women among the crowd of pram-pushers. Indian curiosities like the Globe inflame my imagination, and all at once I notice an excessively handsome dark-skinned woman with jet black eyes actually beckoning me from the latticed windows of the picture palace. She is obviously in trouble. Although I may be knifed at any moment, I go to her assistance: a note flutters from window to pavement. Careless of hostile glances, I open it and read the words, 'Fly if you value your life! The Residency is besieged – the English garrison cannot hold out. . . . Fly!!!' I step back, aghast, on to the corns – the bloody corns, as she informs me in anguish – of a well-upholstered lady intent on her shopping: I have come back to reality, the reality of Upper Richmond Road on Saturday afternoon.

But the night is the time to wander in the London streets, a point made by Dickens, himself a night bird, at the beginning of *The Old Curiosity Shop*. At all times an indifferent sleeper, I have turned wakeful nights to good account by traversing miles of streets in central London and the City, peering up and down greasy alleys, watching the shipping in the docks and eating at all-night coffee stalls. Once I passed a whole night, from midnight until daybreak, in Covent Garden. Noisy at other times, on Saturday night the market is empty, deserted and uncannily quiet under the electric lamps. Down-and-outs break the silence occasionally. They lie down in the gutters in the hope of being taken in by the police from Bow Street – an odd ambition when you reflect on it, that of spending a night in a police cell. About two a.m. an uneasy wind rises, blowing straw and wrapping paper before it and whispering drearily under the portico of the great church, finding its way among the cast iron columns of the market.

Once in my nightly perambulations I came across a perfect Sickert. Naturally the setting was in Camden Town, a glimpse of low life seen through an area railing. An old man in a collarless Union shirt was snoring in a rocking chair down in the basement. An electric bulb, bald as his own head, illuminated him from above. On the table was a half-eaten loaf and a bottle of milk. In the corner by the gas fire, a female displayed her legs, her head being cut off by the window frame. On her legs rested a hand, the infinitely uxorious hand of man. Slowly the hand began to move, and so did I, fearful of an anti-climax. I wondered, as I walked away, if my friends of the Camden basement had been influenced by Sickert's paintings, if it were Nature imitating Art on Oscar Wilde's principle. One can never tell.

An interesting tour of London might take the form of visits to those great houses of Victorian artists; palaces of art left stranded by the ebb of nineteenth-

century taste and money. Several of these – Lord Leighton's and Holman Hunt's, for example – are to be found in Kensington, especially in the Melbury Road area. Others are in St. John's Wood. John MacWhirter's Scots baronial fantasy has only recently disappeared, but the most fantastic still remains though turned into flats – the bizarre Greco-Roman home of Alma-Tadema, whose monogram appears on the gateposts. Beyond the gates, a drive leads to the entrance to this strange residence: the word, 'SALVE', cut in Roman letters, remains on the lintel. The finely moulded brickwork is crumbling in places, and the formal gardens, though the pergola still survives, are not what they were. One can visualize the little Dutchman at his easel in the once gorgeous studio, full of palms, brass and bric-a-brac, at work on yet another mildly anecdotal incident from an idealized Greek life in which the maidens, pensive under branches of oleander or myrtle, are undoubtedly of the 1880 fashion – they were often, in fact, the artist's own daughters; or (the pictures finished in time for sending-in day) one of those 'At Home's' once fashionable among Royal Academicians whose privileged guests were accorded a private view in surroundings suitably rich and strange. Quite possibly the fluctuations of taste have now done their worst as far as the paintings of Alma-Tadema and MacWhirter are concerned; their work, after having been regarded as beneath contempt, seems likely to receive at least a less harsh treatment. But their great palaces of art are destined to remain the strange residuum left by the ebb of Victorian taste, increasingly anomalous monuments to that once-famous institution 'the picture of the year'.

> Yet pull not down my palace towers, that are
> So lightly, beautifully built:
> Perchance I may return with others there
> When I have purged my guilt.

An example of the unexpected pleasures awaiting discovery in London, even in the most unlikely parts, is the Royal Oak inn, Muswell Hill, a pub now being rebuilt. Only a few months ago this tiny, weather-boarded inn stood almost unchanged from the eighteenth century when it was built, but now surrounded on every side by modern semis. Once it stood in a country lane among fields and hedgerows under the shadow of an oak tree. Until quite recently, the ale-house was also a tiny general store. Behind was an overgrown garden full of apple trees and roses, waist high in grass. The bar was the size of the average pantry, or almost, with a diminutive tap room behind, fitted with ancient cupboards stained and grained in yellowy brown. There were scrubbed tables, wooden settles and an aspidistra in the fireplace. The Royal Oak was a beer-house only, but full of genuine character. The ladies' toilet was simply a wooden board with a hole in it, the kind that one sometimes encounters yet in

Soho Square

remote cottages, 'the privy' which, like the fairies, is located at the bottom of the garden.

And, though harder to find, those whose humour it is to make a living from the pavements are likely for some years yet to add interest to the London streets. Only recently I encountered a band of street musicians 'working' (oddly enough) the East End. They were all handicapped in some way or other. I had the time and the curiosity to follow them when they turned into side streets after their Saturday morning's stint. Here, in the back areas, a great and surprising change came over them. The blind man was miraculously restored to sight by the easy method of removing his dark glasses and the 'pad' (the written placard) off his chest. The one-legged man proved, after all, to have the usual number of lower limbs beneath his overcoat and the deaf and dumb one quoth in ringing tones 'Now for the pub!', which was where I subsequently found them in a corner of the private bar, dividing the not inconsiderable revenues of the morning. And sometimes in the East End, on an old bombed site beneath the great, impersonal blocks of flats, you may still encounter Mr. Punch, that old renegade, once again exhibiting his domestic infelicities to his traditional audience.

One of my favourite curiosities in central London is illustrated on the previous page – the Tudor-style gardener's hut in the centre of Soho Square. Did Queen Elizabeth sleep here?

SIX

Shops, Alleys and Markets

———————— ✳ ————————

EVER AN incorrigible shop-window gazer, I adore the London shops, all of them, from the little shops on corners in the East End where rice cakes rub shoulders with bottles of disinfectant and plastic toys to the big department stores and specialized shops for gentlemen in the West End. London shops are at their most attractive in December. Christmas in London is becoming increasingly co-ordinated and sophisticated, but I like the commercialized London Christmas. Woolworths is high on my list of London shops, and I love to wander in these stores, thinking of F. W. Woolworth who was, I believe, so apprehensive of the dentist that his teeth became completely eroded; I like to think of him eating bananas with his gums and playing the organ in his mansion in an American twilight. Christmas at Woolworths is almost better than anywhere else and is announced weeks before in the windows by jocund Father Christmases on pelmets. In the days when I was a small and evil child, Woolworths had their own live Father Christmas, and I remember the sensation caused when, asked by him what I wanted, my reply was, 'To know why you are wearing pin-striped trousers.' The toy stalls, having overflowed their ordinary limits, are full of cuddly dogs, tigers and horses, dolls black, white and brown, old-fashioned boxes of building bricks with a picture on the lid showing you what you can do with them, painting books ('Down on the Farm' and 'Yogi Bear'), mechanical toys, innumerable boxes of games and giant jigsaws. I enjoy the Christmas card counter at Woolworth's – the Strand, Victoria or Oxford Street are much the same; animals, children and rural scenes of the Dingley Dell type are chiefly represented, for Woolworth's know their public; many are of a pietistic nature – starspangled shepherds apparently swathed in bath towels, virgins in multi-coloured robes, pictures of the Pope and others, strongly Catholic, of the kind painted by Raphael Mengs. One can sit at the snack counter (where incidentally is perhaps the best value for money in London) and watch the other customers, whose chewing faces are reflected in mirrors against a background of silvered artificial Christmas trees, paper chains and bells and tinsel angels. Or you can listen to the pop music as you hover over the counters, looking at the paper caps, the decorations, the plastic 'Empire Made' figures from the Bethlehem stable, true descendants of the nineteenth-century Staffordshire groups, the balloons and the frost in push-button spray containers.

Chelsea was omitted, though with reluctance, from the account of London villages, mainly from its being too well known to come within my brief; nevertheless considerable village character remains, or does up to the present, for Chelsea is under attack by the destroyers. Two old shops merit inclusion here, the first especially (illustrated opposite), the fruit and vegetable shop in Sydney Street, a rich example of popular art. Outside in the summer is a sizeable inclined plane of pelargoniums and bedding plants and those opulent hydrangeas that seem to have been specially created to accompany fat aldermen on civic occasions. On the other side are cut flowers and fruit. The shop walls along Britten Street are picked out in brilliant red and blue, giving the effect of a fairground. Climbing roses with leaves curiously like those of the shamrock are painted on the jambs of the door; roses also appear over the window. The shop has an awning made of that artificial grass beloved of undertakers and barrow boys. As I made the drawing, the scene was completed by one of those period Harrods vans – a note of olive green slowly passing with great deportment across the foreground. This is the old Chelsea, the Chelsea of Walter Greaves, who loved to draw such shops, putting in all the characteristic detail, in the days before his self-taught art was permanently damaged by the influence of Whistler.

The other shop worth inspection is the old dairy ornamented with rich tiles and having accommodation for cows at the rear in old Church Street, though it is no longer used for its original purpose.

Lower Marsh, Lambeth, is one of London's most interesting markets and affords a whole morning's unadulterated pleasure. Here you can equip yourself with most of the essentials of life, including long-playing records, car sponges, shell fish, second-hand books, transistors and hedgehog ointment. The last is sold by a gypsy who possesses a rare crystal: he told me once that many persons unknowingly possessed clairvoyant powers, and invited me to try mine. After the crystal cleared, I found I could certainly see a rainbow coloured picture, though it was disappointingly mundane, being only the reflection of a pyramid of toilet rolls on the stall adjoining.

However, one of my favourite shops is in Lower Marsh, a drug store of vintage character. (It is curious how, in the midst of change, certain trades continue to hold to an old-fashioned style of shop and presentation – pharmacies, tobacconists and oil and colour merchants are examples of this conservative tendency.) The Lower Marsh shop has windows displaying cards of patent medicines, dog preparations, soap and herbs. The shop interior is dark and full of character. There is an old wooden counter, showcases full of bottles and bedpans, old

advertisements for hair oil and Cuticura soap. Behind the counter are rows of ancient wooden drawers with pretty, milky-green, glass knobs. Each drawer is lettered in pharmaceutical Latin, some being of rare and intriguing medicaments such as Sang Drac. (Dragon's Blood, a resin once stocked by druggists in the days when they sold artists' pigments) and R. Serpent (Serpentaria Root, also almost obsolete in pharmacy). There are rows of bottles similarly labelled. A bell-push on the counter invites one to ring for attention. Upon a summons, the proprietor emerges from a back parlour, screened from the shop by a charming patterned door of sandblasted glass with, if I remember correctly, the words 'Consulting Room' surrounded by floral decoration, a door that only the Victorians could fashion and every bit as good as the front door of the St. Gothard Cafe, Fulham Road, in the same genre. The drug store stocks cards of toothache tincture prepared by old-established firms of manufacturing chemists, blue backache pills and pills for wind and indigestion. Sufferers from flatulence have, therefore, a double reason for calling here – relief from trouble and the joy of the shop's interior.

The mention of bottles reminds me of one of the most picturesque shops in London, devoted to the sale of empty bottles. This is Marlow's in Barrett Street, Marylebone. Barrett Street is a curious little square with a 'gents' and a pair of once handsome gas lamps, the ornamental cast iron standards being still in position but now electrified in a ridiculous, utterly unfeeling manner. Marlow's bottle shop and the junk man displaying his odds and ends alongside a wall give the place a slight feeling of Montmartre. The shop has kept its early nineteenth-century appearance; add to this its stock of wine bottles of all shapes and sizes, chianti flasks and vats and the result is a visual pleasure of no mean order, particularly when, as so often occurs, the pavement in front of the shop is laid out with crates, sacks and yet more bottles with a coster's barrow or two dotted about for artistic finish. New follies persistently spring up in my mind. One might well invest in some of Marlow's empties – champagne bottles, of course, and those once containing Chateau Yquem – just to deposit in one's dustbin as a means of discomfiting the neighbours, overawing the dustman and filling both with bitterness and despondency.

A favourite London alley might be mentioned here in passing, since it is merely a short walk away – Lancashire Court, behind the former Walker's Galleries (at present a shoe shop) in Bond Street. In fact there is a veritable network of small turnings and alleyways here, most of them of great age. They and the tiny old shops found in them make an agreeable contrast to the fashionably commercialized streets hemming them in. But Bond Street has a high proportion of shops remaining quite unaltered, or at least, if rebuilt, retaining the club-like atmosphere peculiar to the West End. I love the delicate high cast iron windows

WALLERS
DRESSWEAR
SPECIALIST

RECORDS

NEWPORT
COURT

of Aspreys, a corner shop which is one of the most refined in London, and also
Hill's violin shop, also in Bond Street – late Victorian terracotta with rounded
windows and itself as mellow as an old fiddle.

While I was making the drawing of Newport Court (on the previous page), an
Italian appeared, seemingly from nowhere, and promptly set up a gaming booth
which was nothing more elaborate than a camp stool. It was interesting to watch
the way the crowd gathered for this hoariest of dodges – the old three-card trick.
'Anyone can play, find the lucky King, the lucky King out of the other two threes.
Anyone can play. Find the lucky King. . . .' A display of pound notes appeared,
many no doubt tendered by the sprats who are invariably set to catch the macke-
rels, or mugs, in the crowd. I could see no cheating, but the King – the lucky
King – got harder to find; increasingly rapid and dexterous movements of the
hands saw to that. Some put as much as three pounds on a card. A hinged card is
used in the flagrantly rigged games, but it all comes to much the same – the
pound notes deploy into the pocket of the gamester in ratio to the growing shyness
of the King – the lucky King!

Gramophone records old and new, wine, clothes, books and furniture are the
staple trade of Newport Court, which is always thronged with idlers, and at the
top corner a choice selection of idle men are usually to be seen, staring the whole
day through or vaguely reading racing papers.

Lisle Street at the top is less entertaining these days. Time was when one
could always find a friendly face among the frail beauties promenading there,
though a few can still be seen at times. A new problem confronts them as to
whether the sauntering males are interested in Hymen or Hi-fi; the area caters
for both tastes. Some good old houses remain in Newport Court, including one
or two with slightly curved bay windows of the eighteenth century. The furniture
shop in the foreground of the illustration is one of these. In the summer the
windows of the Victorian 'dwellings' in the court are a mass of colour. One might
be in some sunlit, narrow street in Spain or Portugal, so bright are the geraniums
and marigolds, and there are creepers to soften the outlines of the nineteenth-
century brickwork and railing.

The reference to Dragon's Blood a page or two back reminds me of the many
intriguing artists' colourmen once abounding in London. Many of these were
small concerns catering for a specialized market, and could not hope to compete
with the larger, highly organized firms. Newman's, an old-fashioned firm who
made colours for the early watercolour painters, left Soho Square, a distinct loss
to the area. Another was C. E. Clifford who traded in Piccadilly in the days of
hansoms and crossing sweepers. Fortunately a few of the smaller firms remain to
delight the heart. Of these, the most picturesque, perhaps, is Lechertier Barbe's
in Jermyn Street – fine old premises, old showcases, sponges under a glass shade –

Church Street
Edware Road

everything as it should be. Another old firm is Roberson's in Parkway. Here the premises are modern, but you can buy materials quite unobtainable elsewhere. They made colours, brushes and canvases for the Pre-Raphaelites, and, when I first went there, had an old employee who once ground colours for 'Sir John' (Millais), who would never have his Flake White in a metal tube. In those days, one could still buy the most marvellous cake colours of pigments no longer known at ordinary establishments – Smalt Blue, Indian Yellow (real Indian Yellow not the phoney coal tar substitute), Pease's English Ink, Verditer, Dragon's Blood, of course, and many more. I stocked myself up for twenty years ahead, for these colours were the veritable ones used by the men of the great period. Wonderful mahogany boxes could be bought, too, with an engraved lid and stick of Chinese Ink.

This brief list could not be closed without a reference to two more distinctive artists' colourmen – Cornelissen's in Great Queen Street and Brodie and Middleton not far away at the corner of Long Acre. Both have an honest old-fashioned atmosphere about them. Until recently Brodies sold their own watercolours, including such ancient pigments as King's Yellow.

The illustration on the previous page shows the shop at the corner of Church Street and Lisson Grove, an example of the dignified, mildly classical treatment of shop fronts once commonplace in London. Shops of this kind are disappearing fast, but enough remain to remind one of how well these things were managed once, before the feeling for proportion and the habit of doing small things well had quite gone. The adjoining terraces in this part of Church Street above the shops appear to be late eighteenth century or turn of the nineteenth century. The one illustrated seems to have been rebuilt or remodelled early in the Regency period, its balconies on the Lisson Grove elevation being standard London Gothic of the 1820's.

Two other shops of fine quality remained until quite recently in Knox Street, Marylebone, a short distance from Lisson Grove. Both had slightly curved bow fronts with small panes and overhanging wooden cornices and belonged to the earliest years of the nineteenth century. They stood on a site designed for rebuilding; the shop fronts, however, were carefully removed by craftsmen from the London Museum where they are to be preserved.

Yet another attractive shop is Lee's, the newsagents in Gray's Inn Road, one of the few items of interest in that dismal road. This shop is very small and belongs to the late Regency. Two half-columns with Greek honeysuckle ornament at the capitals flank the window, one either side; there are two doors, one with a semi-circular fanlight, and the usual iron balconies occur above. There is nothing in this that could not be done by an ordinary carpenter and plasterer at the time of erection – c. 1825 perhaps – but there is an inherent rightness about

the whole thing that gives satisfaction to the eye and which was nearly always achieved even by the humblest journeyman when working within the framework of the accepted eighteenth-century formulae. Soho also possesses a fine news-agent's shop, but of a much earlier date.

Pullen's, which delighted me in my time at the Slade, has only recently gone from Warren Street. In this instance, the charm lay not in the architecture – though it was good shop architecture of the 1850's – but in the complete period flavour of the whole. There were lace curtains to the windows of the living quarters above the shop, disclosing a variety of pot plants. On the wall between the windows was the large lettered legend 'Fancy Drapers and Outfitters', a completely Victorian title. Bunches of handkerchieves and women's aprons hung by the door. The interior was lined from floor to ceiling with shelves of merchandise – socks, ties, underwear, cloth caps, cards of curlers and hairpins, collar studs. The furnishings consisted of counters and tiers of little wooden drawers, stained and varnished. But the chief delights were the paper collars and paper fronts, those characteristically Victorian shams. Impecunious clerks, desirous of putting on a good show for a minimum outlay, were once the mainstay of the paper collar market; the demand for them today is largely by doctors and other professional men and chauffeurs, all anxious to cut down on laundry bills. Only Victorian minds, at once dreamy and tough, could invent paper neckwear, symbolical, like the water closet, of the inscrutable depths in the minds of Englishmen.

Now one of the most delightful things about London is the number of small firms producing something quite distinct. For instance, there is the firm which makes the Victoria Crosses, the man who tunes the few remaining barrel organs or 'street pianos', the man who made pewter mugs for tourists, giving them the correct antique finish by leaving them out in his yard and bestowing an occasional kick to the pile. I once met a man who spent his life putting worm holes in reproduction furniture. The only cork shop in London known to me belongs to the class of small specialized craftsmen. This is W. Plesents in Clerkenwell Road, where a variety of articles are manufactured out of cork and, of course, corks themselves for bottles of all shapes and sizes. The window, delightfully dusty, has a framed cork picture at the back. This cork picture is typical of its kind – a romantic castle by a lake, a long way after Claude. Specially prepared cardboard mounts could be bought for the reception of these pictures built up in cork – and ready-washed-in skies – when the making of such trifles, very delightful trifles, too, helped to while away the long evenings in the upper-middle-class households of a century ago. In front of the cork Claude is a curious sort of palm tree, hiding behind a glass shade which forms a centrepiece to the window. The glass shade contains a cork model of what at first appears to be a Burmese pagoda but which really represents an English parish church rather freely rendered. A church

notice board, various gable crosses and a clock dispel any uncertainty as to its identity. The church is very individual in design, and must be the only one in London to boast of having three towers and spires – at least of this fanciful construction. Large pieces of the bark of cork-oaks form a decorative frame to the window, the glass of which is boldly lettered in yellow. As can be seen in the drawing on page 99, the entire window is itself a kind of cork picture in a colour scheme of dusty brown, grey and black, with yellow lettering oil-painted on the glass.

But if rarity and richness is your aim, go down to the nightmare landscape of the Elephant, meditate on memories of Quintin Maclean at the organ of the Trocadero and make for Baldwin's, the herbalists, at the beginning of Walworth Road. This shop is a complete cure for the depression caused by the new Elephant and Castle scenery. Baldwin's windows are full of herbal remedies in packets, boxes and bottles. There are dishes of thick Spanish, jars of the twiggy liquorice root (how many schoolchildren chew it nowadays?), dishes of dried herbs, barks, herbal soaps, that excellent Albion milk and sulphur soap once recommended to my family by Sir Thomas Flitcroft, physician to Edward VII, herbs in pill form, in liquid extract or in tablets, ginger, spices and materials for wine making. Entertainment and interest can be measured in square feet in Baldwin's windows. The interior is even better. There are old framed posters and printed announcements – one I seem to remember describing a preparation for cooling the blood of women – a useful remedy, I fancy, in most households. Show cases are crammed with medicaments; there is an old clock and a certificate of merit for dog medicines exhibited at Crufts. Best of all is the marble topped counter behind which is a little 'bar'; here you may cool off your own blood with a glass of sarsaparilla. As might be expected, Baldwin's retain some good old labels, which are in themselves worth the journey, the one on the tin of Indian tooth powder being notably fine. Such shops ought not to be ruined by modernization: in fact, they deserve official protection and a Government grant in exchange for an undertaking never to alter the premises.

The drawing on the previous page illustrates a shop of a kind all but unique in present-day London – a coal shop. There is a type of coal shop in Hoxton, certainly, at the corner of Myrtle Street, but coal is sold only in paper bags, a modern innovation, and they also deal in old shoes, discarded suits and second-hand corsets. The Islington shop takes one immediately back to Victorian London when the working class had to buy coal in ha'porths and pennyworths. At this shop, coal is still bought in small quantities – perhaps not wholly for the same reasons – lack of storage space is one factor today, though money is still short in these London districts. For whatever reason, the customers come. Modest purchases, dug out from heaps of various qualities by the proprietor or his wife, weighed out in the

big scales, are emptied into bags, baskets or sacks and wheeled away, often by small boys pushing ramshackle prams. Old female gnomes, fit subjects for Rembrandt, hook a nose round the door and order a few pounds to be called for later. A woman with a horde of infants, apparently about to increase her collection, asks for her supply to go on the slate: her hubby is on the dole. Coal dust floats in the air, the scene being made harsh by the pitiless glare of unshaded electric bulbs. Questioning, snub-nosed faces of urchins, their mouths edged with cheap raspberry jam, peer through the grimy windows and steam up a patch of fog on the glass. Coal shops were once common in the working-class districts; now they are as exiguous as their one-time labourer, the humble, obsolete cart-horse.

One or two florists' shops can still be found with their conservatories intact in London, though most of their surrounding land has been sold long ago for building. Several of the humbler type florists exist in the unfashionable parts – Greenwich, for instance, Deptford and New Cross. Some have alcoves filled in with bits of rococo-like fretwork painted white; ancient latticework remains in others and pierglasses, spotted and discoloured. In these shops, the cut flowers are kept in decorated jugs of the bedroom washstand kind, and the owner emerges from the inner parlour through a door that goes 'ping' and discloses in the distance a view of Ma's aspidistra. As a foil to these, I illustrate (on the previous page) what I believe is the last retail shop in Covent Garden – Solomon's – a shop splendid with engraved and painted glass, Royal coats-of-arms, mirrors and richly period lettering like that on the fascia. 'Lewis Solomon, Grapevine'.

I drew this shop when the market was overflowing with Christmas goods and the open space in front of St. Paul's a forest of Christmas trees. That is the time of the year to see Covent Garden at its best. Not enough people visit the place at any time. The architecture of the market is original and entirely satisfactory. A fruit and vegetable market had gradually come into being in Covent Garden during the eighteenth century. In 1828, the Duke of Bedford decided to erect permanent quarters for it, and the present building (somewhat altered in the arrangement of roof and internal aisles) was built by Charles Fowler in 1831–33. The Greek Doric colonnade continues round the market, giving unity to the design, but the most pleasing features are the square pavilions on the corners. These once contained shops, that on the south west corner still having its nineteenth-century owner's name, 'Jas. Butler. Herbalist . . . Lavender Water', on the stonework in the square set lettering of the time. Fowler built another market immediately afterwards, the Hungerford Market, demolished to make way for Charing Cross Station. Covent Garden has been the subject of agitation for many years: it is monstrously inefficient, congested and unsuitable for modern traffic conditions. And so it will go and, with it, half the attraction of the northern reaches of the Strand.

Wardrobe
Place
CARTER LANE

The narrow ways and alleys of the City, its odd unexpected turnings, court-yards and passages continually surprise those who believe they know the City intimately; or something previously unknown is stumbled on, perhaps when least expected. All of which is the true reward of those who love to get ever closer to London, to understand a little of its mysteries and changing moods. But only those on familiar terms with the City could believe how quiet it is in Wardrobe Place, Carter Lane, a tree-lined close only a minute from Ludgate Hill and St. Paul's (illustrated on the previous page). You might imagine yourself in the close of some great cathedral, where those eighteenth-century houses would be in-habited by minor canons and the old ladies of the precincts. There would be gaiters, ear trumpets and the little scandals of Barchester. Lacking these, the court has yet a pensive, solemn air about it, companionable and reassuring, and there is a twilight effect even on the brightest afternoon. This feeling of being in a cathedral precincts is more noticeable after the daily inhabitants, solicitors mainly, have gone. Cleaning women are the last to go – those indestructible chars, female John Bulls, whose souls, if examined, would be found dyed with the colour of London – or almost the last, after doing the brass plates, for there is still the tapping of a solitary, unseen typewriter. Soon the typewriter and un-answered telephone cease to trouble. Wardrobe Place has settled down for the night, and is as silent as its sparrows who have gone to roost in their green dormitories in the branches above the pavement.

At intervals the bell of St. Paul's breaks the stillness, chiming the quarters; after the reverberations die away, you can hear the ticking of the clocks in the offices. The brickwork of the eighteenth-century houses is blue-black with the discolouration of years, though geraniums and asparagus ferns add a note or two of colour. The Victorian buildings here are not out of harmony. The King's wardrobe stood in Wardrobe Place before the Great Fire. Today the court is lit only by two gas lamps – one a standard, the other on the wall at the far end. Gradually the light fades and the chambers disappear in dark shadow: it is time to leave before the policeman, coming to try the doors, fixes us with a baleful eye, plainly intimating that we are about to commit a nuisance.

The drawing opposite is of the winding, riverside alley connecting East-cheap with Billingsgate, an alley dark and mysterious, fish impregnated, full of turns and varied contours. Half-way down is the parish church of Billingsgate, St. Mary-at-Hill. Its church tower, of a later date than the rest, has the look of a toy fort, jutting on to the narrow pavement from between the bent and gloomy warehouses. It was at this church that Prebendary Carlile, head of the Church Army, gave his Sunday evening services to the poor of Stepney and similar districts within walking distance of the parish in the years prior to the Great War. These informal services were remarkable for their easy atmosphere and the use

ESSFletcher 196
St Margaret Hill

made of pictures projected from lantern slides, no doubt to the astonishment of the eighteenth-century dead who lay below, more accustomed as they were to drowsy, hour-glass sermons, snuff and learned discourse, all of a piece with the comfortable pews.

The small yards and mews found in all parts of London offer unlimited opportunities for exploration. Crown Passage, St. James's, in homely contrast to its palatial neighbours, is long and narrow, forming a market place of small shops – a barber's shop, a newsagent's, a dairy, tobacconist's, jeweller's, one or two restaurants and a small pub, into which it is next to impossible to gain admittance at lunch time or, having got in, ever to get out again.

Bleeding Heart Yard in Holborn may take its name from a public house, the Bleeding Heart (a curious name derived from the five mysteries of the Rosary, i.e. the heart of the Virgin pierced by five swords) which adjoined. The place was described at length by Dickens in *Little Dorrit*. In those days, Bleeding Heart Yard was inhabited by artisans. Today it is entirely given over to industrial purposes, but worth visiting for the name alone. Goodwin's Court, which connects St. Martin's Lane with Bedfordbury, is one of the rare survivors of the eighteenth century. The bow windows are original, and the houses, now mostly occupied by theatrical firms, have nicely proportioned doors.

Not long ago I had the notion of turning a mews cottage into a studio, an unoriginal but attractive proposition. The more so as I discovered one exactly right – mews below, once the stable of a small greengrocer, cottage above with a pretty staircase and rooms to match. The mews was unfashionable and not in the best part of Kensington, but in all other respects admirable. I was enchanted and about to telephone the agent. Suddenly, from the cottage across the mews, came a down-hearted wail: the unmistakable, unmelodious note of a big trombone, eerie, fearful, fit only for warlocks, banshees and other creatures of Hell. It was Bloomsbury over again – bald head, Oxford shirt, beery nose. This was the end of my studio in a mews.

In a mews off Quex Road, Kilburn High Road, is (or was) a relic of the heyday of the London mews – an announcement for a hackney coach establishment offering 'Broughams, Landaus and Victorias'. The Victoria, a low, light, four-wheeled carriage for two, was really a ladies' vehicle, especially suited to the crinoline. The landau, which was heavier and could be closed or open, was a feature of seaside resorts and their railway station cab ranks ('They also serve who only stand and wait'). The brougham was a one-horse closed carriage, named after its designer, the first Lord Brougham. But the offer is fading from the brick arch and can no longer be taken up: horses and carriages have gone to breakers' and knackers' yards long ago.

The illustration opposite is of Bendall Mews, off Bell Street, Marylebone – a

Bendoll Mews
Marylebone

mews that, although industrialized and given to garages and parked lorries, is yet made most attractive by its group of cottages – Victorian architecture at its most pleasing – unpretentious certainly; within any ordinary builder's capacity at the time, of course, but very agreeable to the eye. These mews cottages are in the main straightforward and utilitarian, though with one or two decorative features, particularly the spiral staircase of cast iron which gives a touch of lightness and elegance. Window boxes appear in the summer in Bendall Mews, home-made affairs gaily painted in green, with red borders and white lozenge panels, and tubs of marigolds, asters and carnations.

Lastly, in this brief account of the subject, is Denbigh Close – formerly Denbigh Mews – Notting Hill. This is a typical London mews, but with rather more architectural pretensions than usual. The stables below are now either garages or converted into workshops for the restoration of antique furniture, for Denbigh Close is off the Portobello Road and an inspection of it can be dovetailed into a happy morning spent among the junk stalls.

Which reminds me of two London markets especially interesting at the end of December – Smithfield, with its own peculiar language and, as it seems, endless perspective of turkeys and other birds for the Christmas table, and Leather Lane. The Lane – if you can edge into it by Gamages – is in a frenzy of buying and selling on Christmas Eve, if a market day. The merchant adventurer needs thick shoes and a well-padded coat: failure to wear this equipment means the loss of several toes and the staving in of the rib cage.

First come the men selling out of suitcases – 'Tinsel, four strings a bob', 'Nylons, shillin' a pair. Pick where you like.' Balloons, all shapes and sizes, also four a bob. After these are the fruit stalls, closely packed with tangerines, American chrysanthemums, cheap jewellery. 'Purses, five shillings, leather, fully lined. Pick where you like. Five shillings any purse and the last few left.' 'No, you can't have a moon rocket, do you think I'm made of money . . . and stop wipin' yer nose on yer cuff.' Now a character with long side whiskers comes into focus: sweets and chocolate are his line, 'Quality Street, seven and three in the shops, my price six bob a tin – last few tins.' Youths and girls press round the record stall, preparing for a pop Christmas. The older type records are left to older type customers – senile men of forty, fuddy-duddy, out-of-touch. 'Harry Tate', shouts the proprietor of the stall, 'Remember Harry Tate?' (Nobody does apparently.) Or, 'The Indian Love Lyrics – anybody want the Indian Love Lyrics? Take them home to your old woman.'

More stalls, more apples, toy stalls, morose men selling wash leathers (wash leathers are not an attractive proposition on Christmas Eve), zip bags, 'Don't forget yer rolled gold tie-pin, yer boot laces.' Near the end of the market, the old Clock Face pub bulges with humanity. This pub is worth a passing glance at least for its lion and unicorn above the door. It is less congested at this end of the market: one can come alongside any desired stall and make fast. As you turn away from Leather Lane towards Bloomsbury and Clerkenwell, its rallying cries still sound in your ears: 'Any size you like . . . any price you like . . . last few left'.

The street markets of Soho are by far the most interesting features of that disappointing quarter. There are a few old courts of tottering eighteenth-century houses, where brothels once had a slippery, illegal existence. I remember years ago serenading the proprietrix of one of these at her top floor establishment on a late spring evening. Madame replied by throwing me a bunch of daffodils, omitting unfortunately to remove them from their jug. Soho's chief attraction, apart from markets, are the dozens of clip-joints and peep clubs, wonderfully boring to all but the deadpan youths and balding, tired men who pay half-a-guinea or more to see a couple of dreary nudes in a quickie show that would be too mild for one's grandmother, uninspiring enough to make a sex maniac go out of business. Nonetheless, the stale, pimply youths at the street door get their clients somehow. It is a rare treat to see the horrid, middle-aged men filing in past the paybox where a vampire collects the cash and then stumbling down dirty stairs, drearily aglow with saucy sex anticipation. This is the best, the only fruity part of the show, and it is free of charge.

If a more old-fashioned commerce is your object and shops which belong to the past, then Battersea offers an almost unexplored territory. Battersea has preserved to the present time more than a few fragments of the old coster life and its accompanying background. This is in spite of a large-scale infiltration by coloured immigrants. A good way to take a sample is to walk towards York Road from Clapham, past the junk shops and old style drapers (all with terraced houses above) and then along York Road. Newsagents abound, fish bars also and small department stores. There is a magnificent jellied eel establishment in Battersea High Street, still with its lamps outside the door and mirrors between the eating boxes inside.

The dusty Victorian streets have a pronounced character. There are long, drab roads of three-storied houses built of sooty brick, each with a scrap of sleazy garden below a grim bay window – grey perspectives dotted with cloth-capped grandpas and fat grandmas: creations after the pattern of Grandma Buggins are as customary here as Rembrandt figures in the Jewish quarter of Amsterdam – eccentric animals with watery eyes and screaming kids. Here is the veritable architecture of Cockaigne, where the only visible concessions to later ideas are the T.V. aerials above the chimney pots. Even horses and carts can be seen in Battersea.

Commercial pressure and high costs are slowly eroding many of the old-fashioned shops of the West End, apart from those officially accepted as of architectural interest, such as Lock's hat shop in St. James's Street or those where the premises have become almost inseparable from the business, only to be divorced from it by risking custom and prestige. Baker Street, which stood in need of all the interest it could muster, has suffered badly from a loss of original and distinctive shops. There was the fine Greek-style pharmacy, handsome and reassuring. This disappeared with the block of which it formed part, along with Elliot and Fry's old shop where, in the rooms above, Charles Keene had a studio. The pharmacy is now lower down in a contemporary manner – pleasing enough as far as these things go, but hardly to be thought of as fine architecture. Whereas its predecessor, the acme of architectural discretion and good manners, was as good a pick-me-up if you had succumbed to the blues as a dose of mist. caffeine fragrans.

Also in Baker Street were the premises of Jou-Jou, the Edwardian corset shop, perhaps the most individual shop of its, or any other, kind in town. When I lived in Gloucester Place, I used to make for Jou-Jou to stare for hours at the period corsets on dummies of a like vintage, the curious announcements in 1920 style lettering and Union Jacks that appeared and disappeared from time to time, apparently of their own accord. And only recently I missed the Edwardian patisserie and tearoom above which had everything except a ladies' orchestra. If this sort of thing goes on, and no one seems able to prevent it, it is hard to see how living in London will be worth while in the future. The evil proportions of the new London blocks stultify the mind, as do their trumpery bits of sculpture or modish mosaic. The thought of what will happen to those destined to live with the stuff, once only the moonshine of hack artists in boys' adventure books but now an oppressive reality, is far too unpleasant for comfort. Still, the developers may be charitable enough to leave a few old shops and alleyways intact, if only to prove how right they were in knocking down all the rest.

SEVEN

Gothic and Graveyards

———————— ✳ ————————

ALTHOUGH I have lived in some few houses of interest and quality in and round London, I have not yet achieved my ambition to own a Gothic one – either in Kew, possessing both a conservatory full of stained glass and a shrubbery, or, for preference, in some absolutely unattractive locality with a distant view over a derelict graveyard. The house would be gloomy inside, full of Gothic furniture and Pre-Raphaelite drawings, and would have a snaky barge board on the gables. From my window, I would stare at the women in plastic macs going to super-market and fish bar, and I would renew acquaintance with Sir Walter Scott and that dreadful Fairchild family whose morals, like those of the Mikado, were particularly correct.

London, so beautifully arranged for life, is curiously ill-fitted, indeed to the point of indifference, to death. A rich man dies and, before he grows cold, his various directorships are occupied by younger, reforming men. A few obituary notices, longer ones in the companies' magazines, a little regret and eternity closes in. He leaves his dull family behind in the comfortable house on the Surrey uplands, even his dog and golf clubs: the doctors have written him off, lawyers and undertakers have stepped in and the rich man is on his way to some fearful, suburban cemetery. Few things in death are more appalling than the tidiness of a well kept cemetery. Thus does London at astonishing speed dispose of its dead. Should his status demand it, the departed will be given a memorial service at a City church. He may be surprised at the number of his friends who fail to turn up. Quite a few will send representatives or excuses, but their own turn will come, such being the economy of the hive. The organ will play 'Jesu Joy of Man's Desiring', somebody will speak of those that are come out of great tribulation and the congregation, their duty done, will step out into the reassuring noise of the street. By tomorrow, the man they commemorated will be as out of date as a flint axe and as prehistoric.

But up to the beginning of the last century, it was considered proper to bury the man in his own London parish, where, if he were wealthy enough, a Mass would be said regularly for his soul: no doubt a superstitious, unhygienic practice, but considerably less grim, it seems to me, than the present one of giving a man his send off by way of a cremation at Golders Green. But the medieval people reckoned without the rise in land values in London and the later horror of the central churchyards (bad enough by the time of Pepys, as can be gathered from his comments on his own parish church) and in consequence found themselves rudely disturbed long before the Resurrection and bundled off. I always think it characteristic of the charity of the present Rector of St. Vedast, Canon Mortlock, who, when the church was restored, had the dead re-interred under the paving of its courtyard in the place where they belonged, refusing to have them dumped in a ghastly cemetery.

Always a collector of morbid experiences, I recently had one of intense melancholy. This was a visit to the vaults of a Wren church in the City, the condition of which was giving rise to anxiety. In order to prepare a report, the engineers had to break into and examine the vaults supporting the church floor and tower. The place was choked with years of burying, since the Great Fire in fact, with the possibility of medieval burials farther down still. The vaults were cold and damp, beetles scurried away from me. The floor was of rubble and dust – thick dust, for the church rests on lime rubble and earth, at least in that portion of the crypt which had been opened. Human bones were everywhere sticking up out of the floor. Skeleton hands were beckoning from the earth in dark, bitter smelling corners. There were piles of broken coffins and lead plates beautifully lettered on the walls of those vaults still unopened. Tea chests were full of mixed human bones – male and female skulls, tarsal and meta-tarsals, with a mouldy pelvis here and there. Some lead coffins were still propped upright on that floor of dust and oyster shell, just as the sexton had left them in the eighteenth century. Perhaps the strangest sensation was when, looking up over a pile of skulls over which the beetles were climbing, I saw the red smudge of a London bus pass across a grating. Those decaying jaws had once sung hymns in the church above, and, clothed with warm flesh, had pressed themselves against each other in the eighteenth century. Those skeleton arms, male and female, had interlocked in tender embraces once, and the sightless eyes that had not the power to blink the offensive, crawling creatures away had once rested on each other in fondness and affection. Morbid imaginings such as these grow rank as graveside weeds in the house of the dead. I therefore lit a cigarette and headed for the Express Dairy.

But I am much attached to wandering in old London burial grounds. They are ideal retreats for meditation and for the reading of certain kinds of literature, such as Sir Thomas Browne's *Religio Medici* and his *Treatise on Urne Buriall*; the stately melancholy of his funereal prose sags like the drooping gravestones, and a pleasing lowness of spirits takes shape in the mind. A suitable graveyard for these reflections is the old burial ground of St. George's, Hanover Square, in

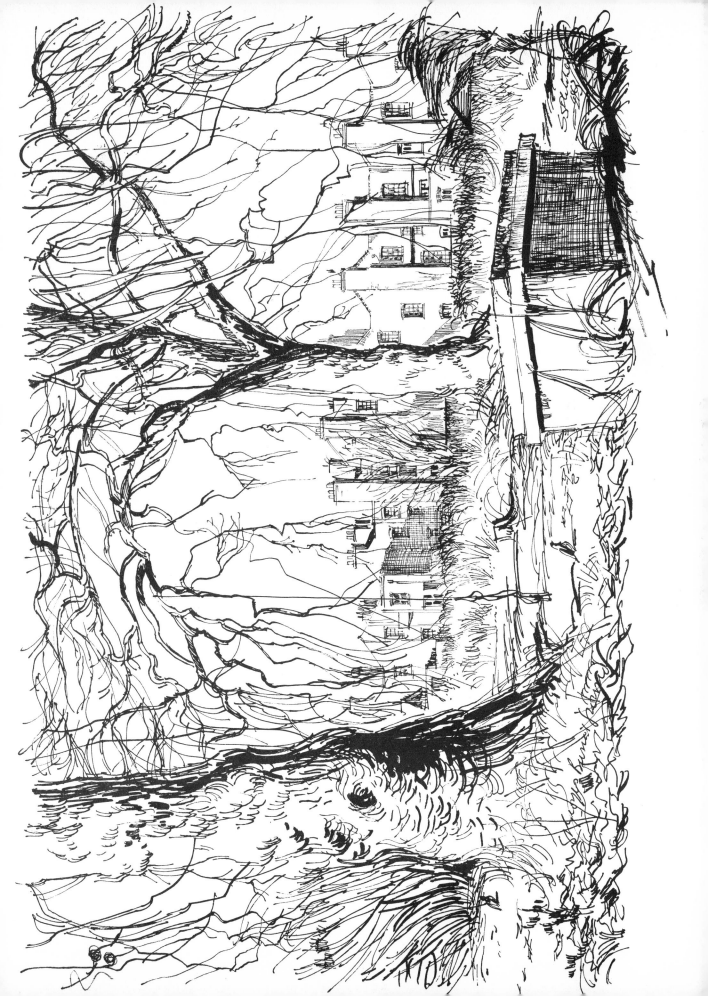

Bayswater, behind the ruined Chapel of the Ascension and consecrated in 1765. At the time of writing, the church is seeking authority to enable the ground to be sold and used for building, for the place was badly disturbed by bombing during the war. Most of the graves are now unidentifiable; the graveyard is largely derelict and the parish without funds for its upkeep. A few fine old plane trees remain. Battered old garden seats, painted a faded blue, lie around in places, and great mounds of earth, overgrown with saplings and brambles, indicate the sites of old, shattered graves. Two interesting tombs remain, that of Paul Sandby, R.A., in the foreground of my illustration on the previous page, and that of Laurence Sterne with the inscription 'Alas, Poor Yorick' on the gravestone.

As I have said, the very neatness of the later cemeteries is somehow more dismaying than the old neglected ones. There can be no sharper contrast than that between Putney Vale and the burial ground in Upper Richmond Road, Putney, an extension of the old parish churchyard consecrated in 1763. The path is overgrown with bluebells and ivy,

> Creeping where grim Death has been
> A rare old plant is the ivy green.

There are dark green vistas, cool in the heat of a summer's day, and a strong scent of flowering plants – cow parsley, hawthorn. Fine tombs are a feature, including an Adam-style one in terra-cotta, and the effect, with sunlight splashing on mossy stone, is like a painting by one of the minor Pre-Raphaelites.

But Brompton Cemetery, that is the place for genteel melancholy if such is your mood! The grim, thick-set entrance is immediately discomposing, needing only the inscription that Dante found over the gate of Hell to set one's mind completely on edge. A brick wall on either side is pierced with arched openings, infilled with cast iron spears. Piranesi could do no more. My drawing was made on a sunny afternoon in June when the lime trees, full of bees, cast a pleasant shade. The burbling of pigeons in chorus with the blackbirds almost overcame the noise of the traffic in Old Brompton Road. Aged men and women sleep on benches in the sun, perhaps in order to accustom themselves to the feel of the place – a sort of dress rehearsal. The cemetery stretches out in long avenues, crossed with lattice work of waving shadow. One tomb has an ordinary door with glass panels to it; half-a-dozen coffins are stacked inside and bunches of long-decayed daffodils and spider's webs; business-like and optimistic as ever, she had spread her snares in the very pit of dissolution.

There are Gothic tombs of the kind illustrated opposite (Gothic and graveyards go well together), Classical monuments and those with doughy, angelic boys. One grave has sculptured figures of a small boy and girl – the boy in a sailor suit and the girl dressed in the fashion of about 1920. Here one may find

Brompton Cemetery.

In loving Memory
of
William Ames Moore
in Hob nes con cur
(JAPAN)
Reshew

the names of foreigners from whom the burden of homesickness has been lifted, people of title laid as low as the rest and military men awaiting Reveille.

Bow is more attractive in these days. There are terraces opposite Bow Road Station that have gone in for blue doors and white paint, bringing a suggestion of Bloomsbury to the East End. Regeneration has gone on in the side streets also, the little streets where the bay windows display a vase of artificial flowers on top of the telly, a place of honour formerly occupied by a cabinet gramophone and an aspidistra. It is through streets of this character that one passes in search of the Tower Hamlets Cemetery. Wellington Way leads to a narrow walk overshadowed by plane trees which seems to have got its bearings wrong and ought to be in Hampstead. On one side is a high brick wall; the trees cast waving patches of blue across it and on the path dappled by the sunlight. Ancient lamp standards occur at intervals. On the other side of the walk are the pillars and corroded iron railings of the cemetery. The cemetery is still used, but the old part is very de-cayed and a visit to it part of the curriculum for all students of melancholia. Saplings have grown through the graves and all round them. Years have passed and the saplings have become mature trees. Rank undergrowth, grown fat on human remains, makes an impassable tangle, as my illustration opposite shows.

The elder, the tree on which Iscariot is said to have hanged himself, flourishes in dim green shadows, leaves rustle restlessly; all dead years, all disastrous things come here as to Swinburne's Garden of Persephone. The very birds are subdued. The grass is arranged in mossy tufts in the manner of the Pre-Raphaelite Arthur Hughes, and mottled by patches of sunlight, deep shades of blue-green dark, swaying emerald, spurts of lemon in the light. Over the rotting graves sail the parachutes of the willowherb to the music of the trains on the Southend line. Slices of bread are discovered among the graves; women's underclothing and fragments of prams, giving additional depth to the oppressive melancholy of the place. . . .

But in the great London cemeteries nothing is, I believe, more mournful than the catacomb in Highgate Old Cemetery in a funebrial Egyptian style designed by Stephen Geary in 1838. One may peer through the grilles at the rows of de-caying coffins. The view of the gasworks through the triumphal arch of Kensal Green is lowering enough, but less so than the Highgate columbarium, which is one of the most frightening places in London.

'And he was afraid, and said, How dreadful is this place! this is none other but the house of God, and this is the gate of heaven'.

Among the famous Victorians to be found here is the gentle Christina Rossetti, whose poetry, itself full of a disturbing melancholy, harmonizes with the char-acter of the necropolis. Karl Marx also lies here; I have often wondered why the Government has never thought of the idea of *selling* him to the Russians in the

YOGI
'BEAR'
FAN
CLUB

Tower Hamlets
Cemetery, Bow

way they sold us the Codex Sinaiticus for £100,000 in the 1930's . . . or, rather than put a price on his head, present him as a gesture of goodwill?

Abney Park Cemetery, Stoke Newington, opened in 1840, was another of the hygienic Metropolitan burial grounds being established at that period. The massive entrance in a sort of Greco-Egyptian style is by William Hosking, who also designed the brick chapel. It is a place of long avenues where poplars rustle in the uneasy wind. There are great pink granite obelisks and an immense number of Victorian statues, single or in groups, tear stained, like the older gravestones, with rain and dirt. The typical work of monumental masons can be studied in detail at Abney Park, prompting the reflection that their sculpture has remained almost unchanged in style since the 1860's. Cork pictures have gone and those of Berlin woolwork, the Gothic Revival has expired, but the type of cemetery sculpture invented by the Victorians – in the sentimental style in popular favour at the time of the Great Exhibition – is still being produced today. In fact, everything to do with interments is strongly Victorian – the wreaths, the insertion of notices in the newspaper and the garb of the undertakers. That life is modern and death Victorian is a curious and stimulating thought and one full of speculative possibilities. There are demure, winged figures, resigned, praying, writing or pointing a finger above; broken columns wreathed with ribands; and here and there are green awnings erected over old graves and newly broken earth – the engineering works by the sappers of the King of Terror. Many of the gravestones have a pair of clasped hands as a symbol of reunion. It is hard to say why this device so distresses the mind.

But the bell of the chapel tolls to remind visitors of the time for closing. They are fortunate in having the power to depart, and move slowly along the avenues, carrying used-up bedding plants and watering cans, to the entrance where the keeper, a trilby-hatted figure smoking a cigarette, holds the keys of the House of Death.

There was a time, now too distant for comfort, when my chief entertainment was the weekly adventures of the Bruin Boys, and I imagined them coming up to London from an unidentifiable suburb (Pinner, perhaps, or Harrow) in order to edit the *Rainbow*. To believe in the impossible is the one privilege of childhood. Their adventures were recorded, I believed, by an artist whose sole task was to follow them around. The reality differed considerably from this, as I found in later years, but only recently have I discovered the actual home of the Bruin Boys, a house of mid-eighteenth century Gothic in the Teddington district (at least I was right about the suburb). The story behind this house of 'Strawberry Hill Gothic' is curious enough. The present owner found the house in a dilapidated state, with grass growing through the floors. Some aged sisters lived there years ago, in surroundings, as I have been told, like those of Miss Havisham – all

Camberley Gothic

cobwebs and dilapidation – and there the old ladies, as part of a team, drew their pictures of the Bruin Boys, often, on fine afternoons, at little drawing tables in the garden. Many of these toy Gothic houses remain in London, often in quarters which have lost caste – Peckham and De Beauvoir Town, near Dalston, for example.

The illustration on the previous page is of one of my cherished specimens of London Gothic – the buildings in Lambeth formerly the premises of Doultons, designed by R. Stark Wilkinson in 1878. Doultons' name can still be seen below the buildings' newer name of South Bank House. Every inch is elaborately orna-mented, niched and fretted. It is the embodiment of high nineteenth-century Gothic at its fullest development. Stylistically the design is a sort of hybrid between St. Pancras Station and the Oxford Museum with G. E. Street thrown in. The work is almost entirely carried out in terracotta, brick and encaustic tile, and demonstrates the permanence of these materials. There is a fantastic door, almost Oriental in feeling, with moulded capitals to the jambs. In the tympanum above is a characteristic piece of Victorian modelling – a highly detailed scene from a pottery, skilfully wrought. A demure Victorian female works on a pot, surrounded by a group of gentlemen in frock coats, bearded and sporting low-crowned bowlers – the kind of men who appear in the background of old public school photographs of the 'sixties. Italianate windows of square-headed form appear along with those of pointed character, and the colour is in what has be-come known as the 'streaky-bacon' style, originating in the writings of Ruskin and Street. Even the chamfered off-sets of the buttresses are patterned.

In *The London Nobody Knows* I described the romantic appearance of St. Pancras seen in an autumn sunset from the rising ground of the Pentonville Road. It is also pleasing on a day of strong sunlight and white clouds, when the whole façade comes to life, made sparkling by shadows cast from innumerable projections: oriel windows, gables, clusters of chimney stacks and Gothic win-dows combine to catch the imagination. One suddenly feels on looking up at the clock tower that Victorian Gothic was absolutely right and that we ought to have gone on building in the style. Much of Scott's Gothic in London – for instance, his baronial Gothic in Dean's Yard – is tepid and mechanical, and the details of the carved ornament lack vitality. But the booking hall of St. Pancras has some curiosities of railway Gothic – capitals carved with engine drivers, contemporary locomotives and the like. Two of these are illustrated opposite. I fancy that few of the millions using the station are aware of their existence. Contemporary figures are of frequent appearance in medieval sculpture, but there is some-thing incongruous in carving Victorian railway men with Gothic foliage, either from the association of ideas or the difficulty presented by a more utilitarian costume. Nonetheless, these few capitals seem to me to symbolize the whole of

Railway Gothic – St Pancras, Booking Hall.

the mid-Victorian age, particularly its strange amalgam of utilitarianism and idealism.

My drawing opposite of the Presbyterian Church of England in Regent Square was made on one of the hottest days of a London summer. A sky like the blue of a majolica vase threw the towers of Bath stone into dazzling relief. Pavements baked in the sun; only a Hindu fakir could walk on them: it was the old June weather of pre-1914 vintage. I have a soft spot for this early Gothic of the Church Building Act period. It has all the attraction of the best amateur art, for in those pre-Pugin days, Gothic was merely one style out of many. Later it became a cause. The Presbyterian Church has towers modelled on those of York Minster. The style is pure wedding cake Gothic, in which crockets appear like cauliflowers, the smaller ones creeping over the dripstones in the manner of caterpillars. The church – originally 'The New National Scotch Church, Sidmouth Street, Grays Inn Rd.' – was built in 1824–7 by Sir William Tite, who later designed the Royal Exchange and had an involved history, being associated at one time, I believe, with Irving, whose great Catholic Apostolic Church still remains in Bloomsbury, turned to other purposes and with its tower unfinished.

Behind the House of St. Barnabas, founded by two nineteenth-century philanthropists as the House of Charity, in Greek Street (incidentally itself of great architectural beauty – splendid with fine carving, plasterwork and one of the finest eighteenth-century staircases in London – once the home of Alderman Richard Beckford) is a delightful and totally unexpected bit of Gothic Revival – the little chapel of St. Barnabas by Joseph Clarke. The chapel is only two bays in depth, but grey marble columns and the use of brown veined stone in the sanctuary give richness to the interior. The stained glass, however, is modern. There are two drawings of the chapel in the entrance hall of the adjoining eighteenth-century house. The design for the exterior shows the dormitories proposed in the original scheme, but only the chapel was built. The Victorians could never resist a touch of pathos, and so the draughtsman has introduced, among the figures, one of a bonneted woman overcome with grief. The drawing of the chapel interior shows a more Byzantine treatment of the apsidal chancel.

One of the most remarkable churches of the Revival in central London is St. Alban-the-Martyr, Holborn, remarkable even by the standards of Butterfield, its architect. Under his hands the resuscitated Gothic forms took on a fresh vitality in a highly idiosyncratic manner. St. Albans was built between 1860 and 1863 to serve what was then a poor working-class area. The church had an elaborately decorated interior, largely destroyed in 1941. In its rebuilt form by A. Gilbert Scott, the surfaces have been kept extremely plain, but St. Peter's Chapel – the Mackonochie Chantry – built in 1890 to the designs of C. H. M. Mileham escaped damage. There is some good stained glass by Kempe, dating from 1885–98, and

Bloomsbury Gothic
Regent Square.

the chapel serves as a reminder of the richness of the interior of St. Alban's before the bombing. Fortunately, Butterfield's western tower with its saddleback roof and central staircase turret also escaped destruction. Look up, past the porch with its motto – 'Free for ever to Christ's Poor. This church is built and endowed in thankful acknowledgement of His mercies by a humble steward of God's bounty 1860' – and the Gothic mood comes immediately upon you . . . there is the beauty of Butterfield's tracery and the quality of the brickwork, red, blue and yellow brick, once harsh and now mellowed by time and the London atmosphere into a harmony of greyish brown . . . until squeaking kids appear from the modern school and the feeling of intense closeness to the 1860's passes like a dream.

Probably the best view of St. Alban's is from Brooke's Market off Leather Lane – a little, tree-lined square with a hint of Montmartre about it. Here the entrance is through the undamaged group of church buildings, looking very much the same as when Butterfield built them; narrow lancet windows, varied in character, and bands of brick and stone are brought together in a masterly arrangement. There is a good corner view to be seen, a group which includes a gas lamp, an Edwardian pillar box and plane trees.

The almshouses of London are fast disappearing; others, such as the Whittington Almshouses on Highgate Hill, entirely delightful, are marked down for future destruction. A notable collection of Gothic and pseudo-Elizabethan almshouses has managed to survive at Penge, at least for the present, for one charming group, the William IV Naval Asylum, is under fire at the time of writing. Another Gothic group, in an advanced state of decay, is illustrated opposite: Alleyn's Almshouses, founded by Edward Alleyn in 1620 in Pest House Lane, now Bath Street, Finsbury. The houses have been rebuilt on two occasions, the present buildings being now almost deserted, though a worn, grey face can be seen on occasions peering through the mullioned windows at the rank grass which forms a meeting place for the dogs of the neighbouring streets and where in summer Finsbury kids attempt to catch those butterflies misguided enough to essay the passage of the streets.

Of all the varied phases of Victorian Gothic found in London, I choose one of its finest examples as a high note on which to end this chapter. This is the Priory Church of Our Lady of the Rosary and St. Dominic, to give its full title, in Southampton Road, off Haverstock Hill. The church was designed by C. A. Buckler and dates from 1874–83.

The exterior of the church gives little indication of the grandeur of the interior, which can best be described as of restrained magnificence. Its colour scheme is pale and sober, mainly in muted whites and greys, the only colour being the stained glass of the polygonal apse: all being carried to just a certain point of rightness and no further. It is hard to do justice to the beauty of the long and high

GOD'S GIFT

Alleyns Almshouses
Finsbury

nave of eight bays receding to the altar, but its effect is singularly impressive. The nave arcade is of tall columns of white stone with stiff-leaved capitals in the manner of early French Gothic. Chapels are ranged along each side of the nave, separated from it by wrought iron screens. These chapels, devoted to various mysteries of the life and Passion of Christ, are in the aisles, and therefore do not interfere with the unity of the church as a whole.

St. Dominic contains much else of interest in the way of nineteenth-century carving and stained glass. There is a fifteenth-century statue of the Virgin, and for those interested in London antiquities, a pillar from the old priory of Black-friars, brought to light when its site was excavated for the building of *The Times* office.

Next to the church are the St. Pancras Almshouses – lawns, canopied doors, beds of roses, Victorian Gothic, the whole group of almshouses and Priory Church being as unlikely a feature of this somewhat depressing area as could be imagined. But surprise and delight when least expected are merely two of a thousand sensations embodied in the magic word 'London'. London! London!